TREES
of HAWAII

TREES
of HAWAI'I

Angela Kay Kepler

A Kolowalu Book
University of Hawaii Press
Honolulu

Library of Congress Cataloging-in-Publication Data
Kepler, Angela Kay, 1943–
    Trees of Hawai'i / Angela Kay Kepler.
        p.   cm. — (A Kolowalu book)
    Includes index.
    ISBN 0–8248–1329–4 (paper)
    1. Trees—Hawaii—Identification.   2.   Shrubs—Hawaii—
Identification.   I.   Title.
QK473.H4K47   1990   90–39868
582.1609969—dc20   CIP

All photos by Angela Kay Kepler except as otherwise noted.

Page i: Coconut palms *(Cocos nucifera)* add tropical splendor
to many island beaches.

Frontispiece: A skyward view through a venerable umbrella-
shaped monkeypod *(Albizia saman)* at spacious Moanalua
Gardens (Honolulu).

CONTENTS

INTRODUCTION

Centuries ago, the Hawaiian Islands were clothed in native vegetation from sea level to a height of 10,000 feet. Sweeping from shorelines to foothills and upward, ground-hugging creepers merged into forests of varying composition and stature, depending on location. These in turn interdigitated with alpine shrublands, high-altitude grasslands, and cindery deserts dotted with silverswords and other specialized plants. Because of the insular and isolated location of Hawai'i in the Pacific Ocean, her original plant life is highly distinctive. Despite a prodigious number of extinctions, a staggering *89 percent of the islands' 960 species of native plants are not found anywhere else in the world!*

With the arrival of the first Polynesians around A.D. 400, the islands' pristine ecosystems began to experience progressive alteration. For fourteen centuries the Hawaiians cleared land for cultivation and burned a considerable amount of forest, especially in leeward areas, in part so that the land would be suitable for growing large amounts of *pili* grass, the Hawaiians' principal thatching material. After Captain Cook arrived in the islands in 1778, newcomers felled more forests, introduced a variety of hoofed mammals (cattle, horses, goats, pigs, deer, and sheep), and altered natural drainage patterns. So immense were the changes that by 1892, Moseley, a naturalist aboard the *Challenger* expedition, observed:

> These islands of the Hawaiian group are most remarkable for the extremely barren aspect which they present as viewed from seawards . . . no trees or shrubs form a feature in the view, but the hill slopes are covered with a scanty clothing of grass and low herbage. Only one scanty grove of Cocoanut-trees is to be seen on the shore of Oahu island, to the east of the town of Honolulu . . . no dense forests clothing the mountains from the summits to the shore as at Fiji. . . .

Missionaries and settlers, from the earliest times, began programs of plant (and bird) introductions. Today, Hawai'i claims first place for the largest number of introduced plants in the world. There are no fewer than 5,000 species of exotics in the islands' populated areas, lowlands, and hill slopes. Landscaping gems have been selected from all over the tropics and subtropics, and there is no doubt that they contribute greatly to the islands' magnetic appeal. The lowlands of Hawai'i are today prettier and greener than they have been for centuries, and each year planned and natural growth enhances this beauty. Tourist destinations such as Honolulu, Wailea (Maui), Kona (Big Island), and Princeville (Kaua'i) are well known for their attractive and well-maintained landscaping. The most common and glamorous of the ornamental trees and shrubs are described in the following pages.

The average visitor or resident sees few native plants, but certain forested areas are accessible to the public (see Appendix for specific locations). In addition, the potential of specialties such as *loulu* (fan) palms, hibiscus, and coastal vegetation is now being realized by some landscapers.

Most of the roadside, garden, and lowland forest vegetation has been introduced from many parts of the world and is different from that found in the continental United States. Ornamentals such as oleander, hibiscus,

1

bougainvillea, and plumeria are nevertheless commonplace in California and Florida. Although some trees and shrubs in Hawai'i may be unfamiliar, do not be overwhelmed; many are easily identified. Smell them, photograph them, admire them. Every flower is a piece of natural art; but some plants are poisonous, so unless you know the plant, do not pick or eat its fruit. Remember that it is illegal to take fruits (except pineapples, coconuts, and treated papayas), rooted plants, and soil to the U.S. mainland, because of agricultural pests.

Over many decades, particularly recently, gargantuan efforts to protect the precious natural heritage of the Hawaiian Islands have been made by the National Park Service, assisted by numerous federal, state, county, and private organizations (such as The Nature Conservancy). Feral pigs, goats, and aggressive introduced plants are particularly destructive. Management efforts will continue in the state's watersheds to maintain forest verdure for the benefit of future generations, to enhance the quality of drinking water, and to improve habitats for numerous endangered species of birds, plants, land snails, and insects.

Grateful thanks to all who shared their enthusiasm and talents during the evolution of this book, especially Derral Herbst, Bob Hobdy, Cameron Kepler, and Paul Weissich.

Whether you live in the islands or only have the opportunity for a short visit, I hope this book will enrich your understanding of, and love for, Hawai'i.

'Ōhi'a lehua trees frame a view of famous Kalalau Valley, Kaua'i.

HOW TO USE THIS BOOK

This book is to help the layperson—both visitor and resident—enjoy the greenery and color that so deeply enhance one's Hawaiian experience. No previous botanical knowledge is necessary. The trees and shrubs described here are those that anyone with curious eyes can spot as they drive around the city and countryside. They have been selected for their attractive or unusual flowers, fruits, leaves, or overall shape. Seasonal changes in flowering, fruiting, and fullness of foliage, as in temperate climes (but less marked due to milder weather), depend on age, degree of ripening, soils, month of year, prevailing winds, general climate, and local weather conditions.

To facilitate identification, the book is divided into seven color-coded sections, each featuring the most conspicuous character of the tree. For example, because the guava tree has small white flowers but relatively large yellow fruits, it can be found in the "yellow" section. If a flower exhibits several color forms, it will be found in each pertinent section. A color band on the top of appropriate pages aids in quick, easy referencing. You may run into trouble with green fruits, depending on whether a particular fruit ripens and changes color (e.g., green papayas turn yellow) or remains green (e.g., false kamani fruits).

If you cannot identify a plant in the color sections, turn to the eighth section, "Inconspicuous Flowers or Fruits," an assemblage of palms, tree ferns, and trees with fewer obvious distinctive characteristics. If this is still insufficient, the state libraries carry a variety of books and scientific publications ranging from gardening topics to treatises on native trees: *The Hawai'i Garden: Tropical Shrubs* and *The Hawai'i Garden: Tropical Exotics* by H. Clay and J. Hubbard (1977), University of Hawaii Press, Honolulu; *Hawaiian Heritage Plants* by A. K. Kepler (1983), Oriental Publishing Company, Honolulu; *Hawaiian Flowers and Flowering Trees* by L. Kuck and R. Tongg (1964), Charles Tuttle Co., Rutland, Vermont; *In Gardens of Hawaii* by M. Neal (1965), Bishop Museum Press, Honolulu; *Plants and Flowers of Hawai'i* by S. Sohmer and R. Gustafson (1987), University of Hawaii Press, Honolulu (native plants only); or for the serious student, *Common Forest Trees of Hawaii* by E. Little and R. Skolmen (1989), USDA Handbook; *The Indigenous Trees of the Hawaiian Islands* by J. Rock (1974), Charles Tuttle Co., Rutland, Vermont; and *Manual of the Flowering Plants of Hawai'i* by W. Wagner, D. Herbst, and S. Sohmer (1990), University of Hawaii Press, Honolulu.

YELLOW FLOWERS OR FRUITS

BANANA
Musa × paradisiaca

An early Polynesian introduction, the banana's long, broad leaves and layered bunches of fruit tipped with purple, heart-shaped "buds" are commonly seen in gardens or growing wild along the highways of each island. Favored varieties for eating are Bluefields, Apple, Chinese, and Williams. Other types are grown for cooking, fiber, or ornament.

Although a staple elsewhere in the tropics, bananas were only minor dietary items for the ancient Hawaiians. In fact, women were forbidden to eat most varieties of bananas.

Attaining 30 to 40 feet in height, banana plants are technically not trees but huge herbs. Their thick, succulent trunks, formed from overlapping, fleshy leaf bases, require huge amounts of water (each plant requires an average of 16 feet of water per year). If you cut one open it resembles a gigantic onion.

Keiki (young plants) require about 18 months to mature and bear fruit, after which the entire trunk is cut down. Suckers from around its base will eventually each bear a bunch of fruit. Insect infestations prevent Hawai'i from exporting fruits overseas, thus banana plantations are not large business enterprises as in many other Pacific islands.

Hawai'i grows only a fraction of its food needs; most supermarket fruit is imported from Central America.

Local plantations on O'ahu flank the Pali Highway (Kailua side) and nestle within wet valleys on the east and south coasts of the Big Island and the north coast of Kaua'i.

Family: Musaceae
Relatives: heliconia, bird of paradise, traveler's tree
Other Names: *ma'ia*
Origin: Southeast Asia

A wild *'iholena* banana plant, North Waiehu Valley, Maui.

Close-up of flowers and developing fruits of Williams hybrid banana.

BE-STILL TREE
Cascabella peruviana

Always appearing partially closed, the be-still's smooth, clear, funnel-shaped flowers (2–3 inches long) generally hang singly from narrow, glossy foliage.

In Hawai'i, this strangely named shrub brightens roadsides, condominiums, and gardens at all elevations.

Like the common oleander to which it is related, all parts are slightly poisonous. If you need a flower for your hair, pluck a nearby hibiscus or plumeria instead.

Family: Apocynaceae
Relatives: plumeria, periwinkle,
***maile*, oleander**
Origin: tropical America

Bright yellow floral funnels adorn the be-still, a hardy but poisonous ornamental.

GOLD TREE
Tabebuia donnell-smithii

Dazzling to the eyes, a gold tree in full bloom (February to June) has few peers. Masses of clustered golden bells burst forth from bare branches, lasting several weeks before leaves appear. Their impact is heightened by the fact that gold trees thrive in hot leeward areas, for example, Līhu'e, Waimea (Kaua'i), Honolulu, and Lahaina (Maui), where bright sunshine adds a sparkling glow to their natural richness.

Branches emerge high off the trunk so that one often looks upward, squint-

Brilliant trumpets of yellow tecoma in October (Honolulu).

ing against bright skies. The original seed was planted at Foster Botanic Garden, Honolulu.

Individual blossoms are shaped like flaring trumpets (2 inches long) fringed with five frilly petals.

Gold trees tend to blend into garden greenery when not flowering. Their leaves are distinctive, having several long (up to 10 inches) leaflets shaped like fingers of a hand.

Gold trees grow near, and are often confused with, golden shower trees (p. 8), which have pea-shaped rather than bell-shaped blossoms.

Even more similar is yellow tecoma *(Tecoma stans),* which also possesses golden, trumpet-shaped flowers. Its leaflets are grayish and it blooms later in the year (summer and fall).

Family: Bignoniaceae
Relatives: pink tecoma, African tulip tree, jacaranda
Other Names: primavera
Origin: southern Arizona, Florida, and South America

A leafless show of gold trees in May (Lahaina, Maui).

A dazzling gold tree in February, Waimea, Kaua'i. (Photo by Robert Hobdy)

GOLDEN SHOWER TREE
Cassia fistula

Voluminous, grapelike clusters of golden "sweet peas" weigh down the branches of this striking ornamental. Blooming from March to August, these trees beautify the islands' lowlands, wet and dry.

Particularly lovely specimens are found in older established towns such as Honolulu, Hilo, Lahaina, and Līhuʻe. Fallen petals lay like yellow carpets.

The leaves are large and divided, with rounded leaflets up to 6 inches long. The long, narrow, cylindrical seedpods (up to 2 feet) contain dozens of seeds, which are sometimes gathered to string leis. Together with the similar rainbow (p. 16), pink, and pink-and-white shower, the golden shower's primary use is to uplift the spirits with glorious color.

Family: Leguminosae
Relatives: monkeypod, *kolomona*
Origin: tropical Asia

Golden shower in July (Lahaina, Maui).

GUAVA
Psidium guajava

In Hawai'i, tasty guava products such as jelly, sherbet, and POG (passion-orange-guava juice) are readily available; some are even marketed on the mainland. Sightseers are often reluctant, however, to pick the guava's lemon-sized fruits that grow wild in countless tons, for fear they may be poisonous. Have a good look at these photographs and eat away as you drive around the islands' rural roads!

Since their introduction in 1791, guavas have spread widely, greedily devouring pastures, gullies, and lowland slopes from sea level to over 3,000 feet elevation. Plentiful in wetter areas on all major islands, they constitute the islands' most abundant foraging

Pink-fleshed, with yellow knobby skin, guavas from moist, sunny areas are tastiest.

Low, wild guava forest flanks Lumaha'i Stream, Kaua'i.

item, primarily in spring and late summer. Fruits vary in quality. Select the large ones, soft but not squishy, that have skin with an overall rounded knobbiness and dark pink flesh. Do respect "No Trespassing" signs, even though most landowners do not mind if you pick guavas along fencelines and roadsides.

Most fruit for commercial purposes is gathered from wild trees, but orchards (especially on Kaua'i) produce guavas year-round. O'ahu, Maui, and the island of Hawai'i have guava processing plants.

The name "guava" is from the Spanish *guayaba* and reflects the plant's native area, tropical America.

Fruit flies, serious pests to fruit industries in Hawai'i and potentially devastating hazards to agriculturalists in California and Florida, love to breed in the guava's soft, sweet pulp.

Family: Myrtaceae
Relatives: eucalyptus, 'ōhi'a, rose apple, strawberry guava
Origin: tropical America (including West Indies)

Looking like lemons, guavas are filled with a pink, sweet-sour pulp, which most people pronounce delicious.

A commercial guava farm, Hanalei Valley, Kaua'i.

HAU
Hibiscus tiliaceus

Rich in Pacific lore, this coastal hibiscus, a tree-*cum*-shrub-*cum*-thicket, is either native or an early Polynesian introduction to Hawai'i. Today, *hau* (rhymes with cow) lines coasts and waterways along the northern wet shores of all islands, even in settled regions. In olden days, its lightweight branches provided cordage, fishing floats, slings, house posts, food strainers, fishing taboo signals, and even fireworks displays. Next time you watch traditional Tahitian dancing, note the girls' swishy "grass" skirts—authentic ones are made from the finely split inner bark of the *hau*.

The tendency of *hau* to form rapidly expanding, impenetrable entanglements has limited its landscaping potential. It loves to stalk on stiltlike branches along and across rivers, for example, the Wailua River on Kaua'i ("Fern Grotto" location) and at Hanalei and Lumaha'i on the north coast. On Maui, trails through *hau* are maintained at the Wailua Wayside Lookout (Hāna Highway near Ke'anae) and Wai'ānapanapa State Park (freshwater caves). Ala Moana Park, Honolulu, has a beachfront *hau* arbor, carefully tamed.

Hau blossoms, ancient symbols of the human soul, are ephemeral. Unfurling yellow in the morning, turning orange in the afternoon, and withering to a dark pinkish orange by nightfall, they are replaced daily.

Hau is similar to, and often confused with, *milo* (p. 14).

Family: Malvaceae
Relatives: *milo*, hibiscus, *'ilima*, okra
Origin: tropical Pacific and Asia

Hau frequently flanks fresh, salt, or brackish waters (Nāhiku, Maui).

Hibiscuslike *hau* flowers, 2–3 inches across, dot its profusion of heart-shaped leaves.

Impenetrable thickets of *hau* challenge even the hardiest hikers (north coast, Kaua'i).

HIBISCUS
Hibiscus spp. (hybrids)

Large yellow cultivars of hibiscus, each lasting two days, decorate gardens and commercial landscaping throughout the state at all inhabited elevations (see pp. 20, 29, 37, 42).

The yellow hibiscus *(H. brackenridgei)* is the state's official flower.

Multihued hybrids up to 6 inches across are common, though a little excessive, as hair adornments.

KOLOMONA
Senna surattensis

Although not native, this "wild shower," an evergreen shrub with lavish, year-round clusters of yellow, pealike flowers, resembles but is not as arresting as the rainbow shower (p. 16).

It carries a Hawaiian name because of its similarity to a native dryland bush called *kolomona (S. gaudichaudii)*, now very rare. The Hawaiians must have named these two *kolomona* after the arrival of the missionaries, as the name means "Solomon."

Widespread in gardens, city parks, highways, and wastelands, particularly on Oʻahu, the ample heaps of "scrambled eggs" and rounded, divided leaflets of *kolomona* are seen also in the pastures and along the roadsides of Kauaʻi and the Big Island.

Family: Leguminosae
Relatives: shower trees, another *kolomona* **with pointed leaves** *(S. septentrionalis)*
Other Names: *kalamona,* **"scrambled eggs" tree**
Origin: Asia to Polynesia

Kolomona brightens Punahou Street, Honolulu.

LOQUAT
Eriobotrya japonica

Loquats, along with *sushi*, summer *bon* dances, and Buddhist temples, remind us of the unique Japanese influences in Hawai'i. Although capable of growing at all elevations on the major islands, these trees, with large, thick, toothed leaves, produce their biggest and tastiest fruit between 3,000 and 5,000 feet elevation.

In winter and early spring, bunches of yellow fruits, approaching the flavor of apricots, are refreshing to eat raw or as jam.

Loquats originated in central China, although they were brought to Hawai'i from Japan, where they have been cultivated for centuries.

Seeds carefully stashed in the pockets of early Japanese immigrants somehow survived the Pacific journey to become established during the late nineteenth century.

Unfortunately, maturing fruits are frequently pierced by one of the islands' introduced nuisances, the Oriental fruit fly. Thus, by ripening time many have been sampled first by either these pesty insects or tiny green birds called white-eyes (mejiros), also Asian imports.

Family: Rosaceae
Relatives: apples, peaches, apricots
Origin: China

These apricotlike delicacies are common at cooler, higher elevations (Kula, Maui).

MILO
Thespesia populnea

Milo (pron. meelo), for visitor and resident alike, conjures up memories of sunny island beaches, parks, coasts, or perhaps one's favorite hotel.

Although occurring naturally elsewhere in the Pacific (its small seeds can withstand up to a year of wave-tossing, then wash up, and germinate in hot sand), *milo* did not reach the isolated Hawaiian archipelago without help from far-traveling Polynesian voyagers.

Milo, having a rich folklore, was esteemed by the Hawaiian *ali'i* (royalty), being particularly favored for the making of large wooden bowls (calabashes). Richly colored, with close, contrasting grains encompassing layers of cream, fawn, tan, and chestnut, all interlaced with swirling pinks, *milo* woodwork, when sensitively carved, is unsurpassed.

Its yellow, hibiscuslike flowers and

Multicolored swirls of *milo* produce elegant, glossy ornaments (Honoka'a, Big Island).

A grove of *milo* beautifies Moanalua Gardens (O'ahu).

glossy, heart-shaped leaves are commonly encountered along island coastlines and in lowland landscaping.
Waikīkī Beach (Oʻahu), Kīhei to
Kāʻanapali (Maui), and Līhuʻe to
Kapaʻa (Kauaʻi) are especially good
locations.

Milo and hau (p. 11) are so closely
related that they are often confused.
Note the darker, shinier, very pointed
leaves of milo, plus seedpods that do
not split open. It also grows as a tree
instead of forming the rambling tangles
of branches typical of hau.

Family: Malvaceae (see hau, p. 11)

Hibiscuslike flowers of milo never open
fully. Note the rounded seedpods, which
never split open (east Molokaʻi coast).

PAPAYA
Carica papaya

Native to South America, papaya was
one of the first fruits introduced to
Hawaiʻi (early 1800s), but it was not
until 1947 that Solo papayas, the pre-
dominant variety grown today, arrived.
Strains developed by the University of
Hawaii's College of Tropical Agricul-
ture are considered the tastiest and
least stringy in the world. Unfortunately, supermarket fruits are picked
too green, and a hot water/fumigation
treatment (mandatory for export),
which controls storage decay and fruit-
fly infestation, diminishes their flavor.
The most scrumptious papayas are
tree-ripened at low elevations amid
plenty of sunshine and rain.

The major papaya orchards are at
Kapoho (Puna District, Big Island). The
palmlike plants are commonly cultivated, and wild ones are especially
noticeable on Molokaʻi (south and east
coasts) and Maui (Hāna to Kīpahulu).

Papayas come in three "sexes":
male, female, and hermaphrodite.
Males produce long-stemmed flower
clusters but no fruit, while females and
hermaphrodites bud off flowers close to
the trunk, which mature into the

Fruits from warm, moist microclimates are
sweetest and tastiest.

familiar round or pear-shaped delicacies. This is a practical consideration for the home gardener. By planting old-fashioned varieties, you risk waiting months to discover if your tree is the "right" or "wrong" sex! If you buy self-pollinating Solo papayas, every seedling bears fruit.

Incidentally, a novel use of the "plumber's helper" (mounted on a long handle) is in harvesting out-of-reach papayas. Push it up and catch the falling fruit with your other hand. Accomplished pickers can "harvest" up to 1,000 pounds of fruit per day with this lowly implement.

Family: Caricaceae
Other Names: pawpaw (British)
Origin: Brazil

Wild papayas, Hālawa Valley, Molokaʻi.

RAINBOW SHOWER TREE
Cassia × nealae

Billowy masses of bright hues from these spreading legumes possess magnetic attraction. On closer investigation their distant fluffy yellowness separates into creams, bronzy yellows, yellows, oranges, pinks, and reds.

No two trees are alike. This variability stems from their hybrid nature: a cross between pink-and-white and golden shower trees. Sometimes the inner and outer petals exhibit different colors, resulting in a two-toned effect.

Leaves are large and fernlike. A named hybrid, the rainbow shower is sterile. Its lack of seedpods results in lower maintenance. The similar golden shower (p. 8), with golden rather than yellow overall color, blooms in summer but rarely beyond September.

The official tree of the City of Honolulu, the rainbow shower cannot be missed in this beautifully landscaped metropolis. They line streets, beautify parks, and shade buildings. As if from a fairy's wand, this dazzling floral outburst (June to October) magically transforms dull corners of the city into treasure spots. Enjoy them along the H-1 freeway and Kapi'olani Park (O'ahu), at the Lahaina Jodo Mission and in Hāna (Maui), and throughout Hilo (Big Island) and Līhu'e (Kaua'i).

Family: Leguminosae
Relatives: pink shower, *kolomona*, monkeypod
Origin: cultivated hybrid with tropical Asian parentage

The rainbow shower's masses of yellow and pink pea-shaped flowers are particularly common in Honolulu.

A magnificent September outburst of floral energy from a rainbow shower (Hāna Medical Center, Maui).

ROSE APPLE
Syzygium jambos

Present on all major islands in wet areas, rose apple fruits are almost indescribable. The size of a lime, their flesh is firm, slightly stringy, and roselike in flavor. Don't disdain the overripe or bruised ones—they are the sweetest.

During the first half of the year, fluffy cream-colored flowers adorn the tree's masses of long, dark, glossy, elliptical leaves. Each blossom is a powder puff of long stamens exuding a delightfully sweet perfume (its tiny

Pinkish and guava-sized, rose apples have a unique flavor (Hāna, Maui, in September).

petals are barely visible). Pick one, though, and by next morning it will have degenerated into a mass of flaccid, spaghettilike strands lying in loose piles under your vase. Present on all major islands in wet areas, rose apples are most conspicuous along the Hāna Highway (Maui), where their abundance characterizes the newly evolving lowland forests. Almost every seed that falls sprouts. Within rose apple thickets, where dense, full foliage creates a shady gloom, millions of seedlings carpet the ground, crowding out almost all other plant life.

In Hawai'i, rose apples have no folklore; they have only grown here for about 160 years. Hawaiians did, however, assign them an appropriate name, *'ōhi'a loke* ("rosy *'ōhi'a*"), referring to both the roselike odor and the similarity of their flowers to the native forest tree, *'ōhi'a lehua* (p. 31).

Family: Myrtaceae
Relatives: eucalyptus, guava, *'ōhi'a lehua*, mountain apple
Origin: tropical Asia

Fluffy, creamy yellow pompons brighten the rose apple's long, dark foliage in Huelo, Maui.

A pretty form of the most abundant forest tree in Hawai'i, the yellow *'ōhi'a lehua* blossom is similar to the rose apple flower. Its leaves are distinctly rounded (rather than long and pointed) and it is not common. You can see the yellow *'ōhi'a lehua* while driving north of Hilo (Big Island).

PINK FLOWERS

BOUGAINVILLEA
Bougainvillea spp. (and varieties)

This flamboyant, adaptable climbing bush graces practically every hotel, park, and roadside in Hawai'i up to approximately 4,000 feet elevation. Over the past 150 years, its splendid masses of color have done much to enrich the beauty and brilliance of gardens and commercial landscaping in the islands.

A native of Brazil, bougainvillea (pron. boo-gan-vill-ee-ah) was discovered by the French navigator Louis Bougainville. Horticulturists have had a heyday with the original purple variety, producing a kaleidoscope of colors: red, orange, yellow, white, pink, brick

Close-up of bougainvillea, showing tiny white flowers and surrounding colored bracts (modified leaves).

red, magenta, and the popular rainbow (an orange, pink, and red mix). They may be single- or double-flowered.

Though requiring heavy pruning, bougainvillea is a year-round trademark of tropical splendor. Its drought resistance, ability to thrive in poor soils, and ease of care enhance its usefulness on arid roadcuts or beside barren lava fields, for example, at Kona (Big Island), Kāʻanapali (Maui), and Līhuʻe (Kauaʻi), and along Oʻahu freeways.

The color of bougainvilleas (like heliconias) is not from the color of the petals, as in most flowers, but of brightly colored modified leaves (bracts) that surround tiny white, tubular flowers. Examine some "flowers" with white centers and this will be immediately apparent. Leis are made by snipping off 80–100 short stemlets of colored bracts, flattening a few at a time so that they rest together vertically, then running a needle and thread through them.

Family: Nyctaginaceae
Relatives: four o'clock
Origin: Brazil

HIBISCUS
Hibiscus spp. (hybrids)

On Kaua'i, one variety of single pink hibiscus is widespread along roadsides, in beach parks, and in private gardens. One of Maui's native hibiscus, *'akiohala (Hibiscus youngianus)*, is of interest ethnobotanically. This erect shrub, whose flowers are composed of a gentle swirl of lavendar-pink petals surrounding a maroon "eye," sports heart-shaped, sandpapery leaves. In olden days this species aided pregnancy: along with taro and sweet potato greens, it was reputed "to make whole and firm the body of the child." Buds from many species and varieties were gentle remedies for constipation, and even today you might find an old-timer *(kama'āina)* treating boils with hibiscus buds pounded with salt.

Single- and double-flowered hibiscus, of colors ranging from pastel pink to rich velvety rose, may be spotted in island gardens (see pp. 12, 29, 37, 42).

MONKEYPOD
Albizia saman

Bursting forth annually with innumerable pink, powder-puff blossoms and lacy leaves, monkeypods have been favorite ornamentals in Hawai'i for well over a century. Even back in 1915, naturalist W. A. Bryan commented that they "occupied almost every yard and square about the city [Honolulu]" and that specimens spreading shade over a space 150 feet across were common on all islands.

The tree's foliage "sleeps" at night. In this regard, Bryan also noted that "After sunset, it presents a wilted appearance and does much toward changing the aspect of the whole city after nightfall." Those were the days

Two-inch pink "shaving brushes" bespeckle the monkeypod's fernlike foliage (Hāna, Maui).

Many stately, spreading monkeypods shade long-established residences such as the home of the Cookes, an early missionary family (Mānoa Valley, O'ahu).

when Honolulu was dominated by vegetation rather than concrete.

Monkeypods are grandiose. Whether perfectly symmetrical domes set amid spacious parks (Moanalua Gardens [Route 78 near the airport] and Kapiʻolani Park, Oʻahu; Queen Liliʻuokalani Park in Hilo on the Big Island), or in rambling pastures (Hāna–Kīpahulu on Maui and the south coast of Molokaʻi), shading streets (Kapiʻolani Boulevard near Ala Moana Shopping Center; Punahou Street, Honolulu; Pākī Street, Waikīkī, Oʻahu; Puʻunēnē Avenue, Maui), or distributed around city and country, their characteristically twisting branches and rounded, umbrellalike canopies lend great charm to the islands' greenery.

Monkeypod bowls and carvings, with their appealing variegated colors, texture, and grain, are popular gift items. Most available for sale in Hawaiʻi are imported from the Philippine Islands.

Family: Leguminosae
Relatives: shower trees
Other Names: rain tree
Origin: South America

Some monkeypods are enormous, with an immense network of branches, twigs, and leaves (Moanalua Gardens, Oʻahu).

Veteran monkeypods also occur in well-used pastures along rural roadsides. Note the natural umbrella shape of these along the south coast of Molokaʻi.

OLEANDER
Nerium oleander

Oleanders, both single- and double-flowered forms, are known to almost everyone, as they are grown in many areas with mild winters, for example, California, Florida, and Australia.

Introduced into Hawai'i before 1875, oleander is a tallish, evergreen shrub whose numerous stems (most of which emerge from ground level) bear slender, pointed, dull green leaves. Most flower continuously with delightfully sweet-scented pink or white blossoms. Tolerating much neglect, oleander is a prime candidate for the beautification of roads and freeways (e.g., H-1 and H-2 on O'ahu), airports, shopping centers, condominiums, and private gardens.

Behind oleander's fragrant sweetness lurk potentially treacherous compounds, cardiac glycosides. These are potent poisons that act directly on the heart, although symptoms vary. The age of a particular plant or of a leaf ingested, the amount of recent rain, a person's age, and other factors contribute to whether you feel sick or die. These complex chemicals even poison honey manufactured from the flowers. And don't even *think* of cutting oleander stems to barbecue hot dogs!

Single pink oleander (double pink is darker).

Family: Apocynaceae
Relatives: plumeria, allamanda, periwinkle, be-still tree
Other Names: 'oleana
Origin: southern Europe to Japan

ORCHID TREE
Bauhinia spp.

Orchid trees, occurring in pinks, mauves, and whites, lend elegance to gardens. They are unrelated to true orchids (see also p. 50).

PINK PLUMERIA
Plumeria rubra

Pink plumeria is one of the many species and varieties of plumeria that enrich the garden and roadside beauty of Hawai'i (see p. 39).

PINK SHOWER TREE
Cassia spp.

Both the pink shower (*Cassia grandis*, Central America) and pink-and-white shower (*C. javanica*, Asia) are showy summer bloomers that bear masses of brilliant pink "sweet peas" and pretty, fernlike foliage. Flowers of the latter occur in larger and more drooping clusters than the former. They resemble other shower trees (pp. 8, 16). Look for them in Honolulu, Waikīkī, and Kāne'ohe (O'ahu) and from Līhu'e to Kapa'a (Kaua'i).

PINK TECOMA
Tabebuia rosea

Pinkish lavender, crinkly, tubular blossoms adorn this medium-sized tree, which blooms all year though not always in profusion. Although not as spectacular as shower trees, pink tecoma's contained shape, resistance to dryness, and ease of care make it a popular denizen of shopping centers, highways, parks, and parking lots throughout the state. Look for them along Nuʻuanu Avenue (en route to the Pali) and Beretania Street (Oʻahu), and at Maui Mall (Kahului, Maui).

   Approximately a dozen other trumpet trees (pink or yellow flowered) have been introduced into Hawaiʻi (see pp. 6–7, yellow tecoma and gold tree).

Family: Bignoniaceae
Relatives: gold tree, African tulip tree, jacaranda
Other Names: trumpet tree, *roble blanco*, pink *poui*, white cedar
Origin: tropical America

Somewhat resembling petunias, pink tecoma's flowers brighten parking lots and roads throughout the state.

ROSE-FLOWERED JATROPHA
Jatropha integerrima

Cheery, rose-colored clusters of flowers (each with five rounded petals and a yellow center) adorn these small, dainty trees, which can often be seen in concrete planters dotting parking lots. Slender, shapely, and willing to withstand confinement, jatrophas beautify shopping areas, banks, hotels, and gardens on every island. They may be rotated with other ornamentals, for example, at Ala Moana Shopping Center in Honolulu. A general rule is: small trees in concrete planters with dark pink flowers are jatrophas; with orange flowers, *kou* (p. 43).

   Especially lush (up to 20 feet high), jatrophas can also be seen in Hāna–Kīpahulu, Maui, and Princeville, Kauaʻi.

Family: Euphorbiaceae
Relatives: *kukui*, poinsettia
Origin: Cuba

Clusters of pink jatropha blossoms enliven shopping malls, city streets, and residences throughout Hawaiʻi.

RED FLOWERS OR FRUITS

CHENILLE PLANT
Acalypha hispida

An uncommon, unusual shrub, chenille plant is unmistakable. It bears long, velvety red spikes that feel like chenille. Under lush conditions, such as in Hāna (Maui) or Mānoa Valley (Oʻahu), these "monkey tails"—actually masses of tiny flowers with no petals—attain 18 inches in length and attractively drape the tall shrub, like Christmas ornaments.

Also look for chenille plants at Foster Botanic Garden (Oʻahu) and Helani Gardens (Hāna, Maui).

Family: Euphorbiaceae
Relatives: Jacob's coat, *kukui*, poinsettia
Origin: East Indies

CHRISTMAS BERRY
Schinus terebinthifolius

Family: Anacardiaceae
Relatives: cashew nut, California pepper tree, poison oak, poison ivy, mango
Other Names: *wilelaiki*
Origin: South America

Since red-berried holly is rare in Hawaiʻi, it has become traditional to gather the dense, bountiful clusters of bright red berries from this shrub/tree for holiday decorations. Fashioned into wreaths, floral arrangements, or hat leis, they last indoors for several weeks. Do be aware, however, that all parts of the plant are slightly poisonous. As with its relatives, such as poison ivy, some people are more allergic to Christmas berry than others.

Common in pastures, along roadsides, flanking pineapple fields, and occasionally in gardens, Christmas berries are most conspicuous from October to December. Their weedy nature makes them highly tolerant of drought and neglect.

Bright red Christmas berries from roadsides brighten holiday hats and homes in Hawaiʻi.

CORAL TREE
Erythrina spp.

Thriving in both wet and dry areas (low elevation only), a few species of coral trees, with their dazzling red, white, or orange clusters of elegant, curved blossoms, invariably attract attention. Up to 12 inches long, these flower clusters burst forth from bare branches during the cooler months.

In ancient times, the preferred wood for surfboards was that of the native coral tree, *wiliwili (E. sandwicensis)*, an odd-looking deciduous tree with swollen trunk and poisonous sap that is particularly common on the desert-like, lava-strewn, leeward slopes of Haleakalā, Maui.

Family: Leguminosae
Relatives: peas, native *wiliwili*
Other Names: tiger's claw, *wiliwili haole*
Origin: Africa, tropical America, Pacific islands

A common myna gleans insects from the coral tree's brilliant red flowers in Honolulu. In early spring, trees are leafless but bursting with colorful "tiger's claws." (Photo by Timothy Burr)

Coral trees line a golden beach (Kaluako'i Resort, Moloka'i).

HIBISCUS
Hibiscus spp. and hybrids

Adorning brochures, posters, and every tidbit of literature pertaining to Hawai'i, hibiscus is universally known. With luxury hotels, golden beaches, sunshine, and coconut palms as allies, hibiscus flowers literally epitomize the islands.

Although thousands of species, varieties, and cultivars exist in every color and hue, lining roadsides, adorning airports, and growing in practically everyone's garden, the ubiquitous red (Chinese) hibiscus is most familiar.

Introduced from Asia around the middle of the last century, this adaptable perennial, with its brightness, profusion of blossoms, and high potential for hybridizing, quickly became popular in the islands.

Despite today's poster image of maidens bathing half naked in mountain pools, sporting red hibiscus flowers in their long tresses, this was not typical of old Hawai'i. Hibiscuses were cultivated and used mainly to enhance greenery or for medicinal purposes.

Hibiscus flowers do not require water after picking and will last a day or two in flower arrangements. They make superb hair adornments or decorations strewn around tables, stages, etc. They crush easily, staining clothing, and so make poor leis.

Several species of native red hibiscus, very rare in the wild, may be seen in botanical gardens that specialize in native plants: National Tropical Botanical Garden (Kaua'i), Waimea Falls Arboretum (O'ahu), and Maui Botanical Garden (Maui Zoo).

Family: Malvaceae
Relatives: *'ilima, hau, milo,* okra, hollyhock
Origin: warm regions worldwide

Cheery red hibiscus are ubiquitous in Hawai'i.

LIPSTICK PLANT
Bixa orellana

The lipstick plant is a small ornamental tree, easily spotted by its prickly red or brown clustered seedpods. During summer roselike pink flowers (with lavender stamens) adorn the tree and later develop into the curious seedpods. Their numerous scarlet seeds were formerly used as the chief source of a vitamin A–rich orange dye for cheeses, butter, and margarine. They make unusual Christmas decorations. Red seeds are often poisonous but these are not.

Lipstick plants are widespread in Hawai'i, mostly in private gardens. Foster Botanic Garden (Honolulu) and Hilo Hospital (Big Island) are reliable spots to find them.

Family: Bixaceae
Other Names: anatto, arnotto,
achiote, blood tree, *'alaea*
Origin: tropical America

Bright, prickly lipstick plant seedpods (Hilo, Big Island).

OCTOPUS TREE
Schefflera actinophylla

Long, red, bulbous arms of the octopus tree are tropical curiosities, common in lowland Hawai'i.

Long floral arms mimicking those of an octopus radiate from the octopus tree's crown. Botanical resemblances to the lowly invertebrate are heightened by the rows of clustered red flowers echoing lines of suckerlike prominences. Given such an unconventional array of flowers, is it not fitting that this sparsely branched tree hails from Australia, the land of floral and faunal curiosities?

Ubiquitous in the lowlands of Hawai'i, the tree's large, umbrella-shaped, radially divided leaves lend a tropical effect to city, garden, and *lānai* (porch). You cannot miss them in Honolulu: H-1 freeway, Nu'uanu Avenue, Mānoa Valley, Kalākaua Avenue (Waikīkī), around hotels, and elsewhere. They are particularly prominent at Kā'anapali (Maui) and inhabit lowland forests on all islands.

Family: Araliaceae
Relatives: ginseng, panax, 'ōlapa
Other Names: umbrella tree, schefflera
Origin: Australia and New Guinea

'ŌHI'A LEHUA
Metrosideros polymorpha

Forests of 'ōhi'a (pron. oh-*hee*-ah) *lehua*, the most abundant native tree in Hawai'i, can be seen from an airplane or helicopter, clothing mountains and imparting to them a distinctive island flavor.

On the Big Island and Kaua'i are areas where its twisted gray branches,

'Ōhi'a trees in the misty forests of Waikamoi Preserve (Maui).

The official flower of the Big Island, *lehua* blossoms are common in Hawaii Volcanoes National Park (Big Island).

Reaching out proudly over untouched virgin forest, *'ōhi'a* branches accentuate the rugged topography of Pelekunu Valley, Moloka'i.

rounded foliage, and bright red pompons dominate roadside vegetation, for example, Hilo to Hawaii National Park, Saddle Road (Big Island), and Kōke'e to Kalalau Lookout (Kaua'i). Here also one can find native birds such as *'apapane*, *'i'iwi*, and *'amahiki*, whose principal sustenance comes from *'ōhi'a* trees. Note the presence of *'ōhi'a lehua* whenever you are above 3,000 feet elevation.

The adaptable *'ōhi'a lehua* (its scientific name *polymorpha* means "many forms") germinates on bare lava, attains a mature 4-inch height in water-sodden bogs, yet also forms rich forest canopies up to 100 feet high!

The Hawaiian name *lehua*, applied only to the flower of an *'ōhi'a lehua* tree, means "hair," recalling the many conspicuous, hairlike filaments (actually long red stamens). *Lehua* is the flower representing the Big Island and has long been used there to fashion red leis. *'Ōhi'a lehua*, sacred in olden days despite its abundance, was used only for carving temple images and war gods. One could be killed for using it for other purposes or, in extreme cases, even if a tree fell on one's property!

Although the name of this species is generally shortened to *'ōhi'a*, several other plants, both native and introduced, also include *'ōhi'a* as part of their name. Examples are *'ōhi'a loke* (rose apple, p. 17) and *'ōhi'a 'ai* (mountain apple, which I treated in *Hawaiian Heritage Plants*). Most are related botanically, thus representing a highly evolved folk taxonomy for which the ancient Hawaiians must be commended.

Family: Myrtaceae
Relatives: rose apple, guava,
    eucalyptus
Origin: Hawai'i

A pioneer on a bare lava flow dating from 1859 (Big Island). (Photo by Cameron Kepler)

ROYAL POINCIANA
Delonix regia

Royal poinciana, flame tree, flamboyant, and peacock flower: such florid names mirror the resplendent display of the islands' most gaudy ornamental tree. Even its scientific name means "regal talons," hinting at the clawed nature of the poinciana's five crimson petals. Umbrella-shaped, it is laden either with dazzling red clumps of flowers (March to October, peaking in summer); lacy, fernlike foliage; or long, brown seedpods (1½ by 15 inches), depending on the time of year.

One's first impression of the royal poinciana is of an elegantly spreading tree with graceful, arching branches that sweep toward and sometimes touch the ground. This classy, small ornamental, native to Madagascar, was introduced into Hawai'i in 1855.

Now present on all islands, it is particularly abundant in Honolulu: at the airport, along H-1 freeway and other city roads, residential areas (particularly Mānoa Valley), and at the University of Hawaii.

Poinciana's 3- to 4-inch blossoms, though stunning, are too brittle for leis but make marvelous hair ornaments. Its dark brown, narrow seeds are strung into attractive seed leis.

Family: Leguminosae
Relatives: shower trees, peas
Origin: Madagascar

Splendid, claw-shaped royal poinciana blossoms (Honolulu).

A shapely royal poinciana enhances the spacious garden around cottages at the Royal Lahaina Resort (Maui).

STRAWBERRY GUAVA
Psidium cattleianum

Bite-size, rich-tasting, sweet, and not too acidic, strawberry guavas are easily devoured by the handful. They are found either in gardens, along rural roads, or along the islands' lower mountain slopes. Although tasty and seemingly innocuous, strawberry guavas, along with common guavas, overrun pastures, gullies, and mountain slopes up to 4,000 feet elevation.

Scientists have found that their seeds, when carried inside a wild pig for a few days and then ejected, germinate more readily than seeds left on their own. No wonder! Each stony seed, softened by digestive juices, sits in a bed of soft manure, which is all ready to fertilize the baby seedling!

Their leaves are 1 to 2 inches long, oval, glossy, and pointed at the tips.

Strawberry guava fruits (no relation to true strawberries) are most common during the fall months in wet regions of neighbor islands, for example, Hāna Highway (Maui) or Hāmākua Coast Road (Big Island).

Family: Myrtaceae
Relatives: eucalyptus, 'ōhi'a lehua
Other Names: *waiawī* (yellow and red forms)
Origin: Brazil

Strawberry guavas, sweet, red-purple snacks from the wilds of Hawai'i, are good either fresh or made into jam. (Photo by Cameron Kepler)

TI
Cordyline fruticosa

The many cultivars of *ti* (pron. tee) are used for ornamental purposes in Hawai'i. Many have pinkish-red, streaked leaves, others have wavy edges, while some are dwarfed. In season, their sprays of red berries are eye-catching.

See p. 80 for the common, Polynesian-introduced, green-leaved *ti*.

Sunlight through red *ti* leaves. Lyon Arboretum (O'ahu) houses a large collection of cultivated *ti* plants.

Cultivated *ti* plants, showing red berries. Berries form more frequently on the domestic rather than wild varieties.

TURK'S CAP
Malvaviscus penduliflorus

The flowers of this shrubby garden ornamental are reminiscent of small, 1- to 2-inch folded umbrellas or red hibiscus buds that forgot to open. It is hardy and thrives in wayside parks and abandoned grassy roadsides, especially in wet areas.

Family: Malvaceae
Relatives: hibiscus, 'ilima, hau
Origin: tropical America

Turk's cap (Kahului, Maui).

WHITE FLOWERS

ANGEL'S TRUMPET
Brugmansia candida

Blooming in island gardens and, rarely, in lush, wild valleys, the attractive angel's trumpet is noted for its huge, bell-shaped flowers (up to 10 inches long), which resemble an old-fashioned gramophone speaker. Colors are white or pale apricot. Their enticing smell can pervade entire gardens on a warm night.

The flower's flared shape indeed resembles a trumpet, but it is also well to note that if you ingest any part of the plant you may be preparing to trumpet with the angels! Wash your hands after touching it.

Family: Solanaceae
Relatives: tomato, deadly nightshade
Origin: Peru, Chile

Large angel's trumpets bloom all year, embellishing island gardens with their enticing fragrance and pastel colors.

BOUGAINVILLEA
Bougainvillea glabra

White bougainvillea is a cultivated form of the common colored varieties: purple (p. 47), pink, magenta (p. 19), and orange.

Less common than the colored varieties, white bougainvillea looks best in a mixed hedge (Lahaina, Maui).

HIBISCUS
Hibiscus spp.

Native to the islands, two species of white hibiscus *(Hibiscus waimeae, H. arnottianus)*, with their exquisite mellow fragrance (rare among hibiscus), deserve special mention. Their large, brilliant white petals (*ke'oke'o* or "white-white" in Hawaiian) surround long, red, central columns.

Rare in the wild (O'ahu, Kaua'i), the genetic material of these species has a century-old history of hybridization

An introduced variety of white hibiscus (Lahaina, Maui).

and cultivation. They dot island gardens and may also be seen at Lyon Arboretum (Oʻahu), National Tropical Botanical Garden (Kauaʻi), and Maui Botanical Garden (Maui Zoo). The smallish white hibiscuses sometimes planted as hedges are an introduced species.

A native white hibiscus *(Hibiscus arnottianus)* thrives under cultivation *(above)* but is rare in the windswept upper valleys of Oʻahu's Koʻolau Mountains *(right).*

OLEANDER
Nerium oleander

Single white oleander is a form of the common pink oleander (p. 24).

PLUMERIA

Plumeria spp.

The simple beauty and sentimental fragrance of plumeria blossoms bespeak the popular tropical connotations of Hawai'i: balmy nights, full moons seen through coconut palms, serenading ukuleles, and lush aromatic gardens. Practically from the moment one disembarks from the airplane, one spots plumerias, either white with yellow centers, pink (p. 25), apricot, yellow, or maroon, beautifying roadsides, residences, condos, and hotels, up to about 3,000 feet elevation.

Introduced in the last century, plumerias were first planted around cemeteries, hence their original name, "graveyard tree." Until relatively recently, local people shied away from wearing plumeria leis because of this association with death. Today they have become one of the most popular and readily available lei in the islands. To make a lei, thread a regular needle and thick thread (crochet is good) through the open ends of the flowers for single garlands (approx. 45 flowers) or through their bases for thick, triple leis (approx. 300 flowers).

Other floral creations include long garlands festooning gardens, tables, churches; low flower arrangements using clusters of blossoms and buds; single flowers threaded on stiffish "wires" made from the stiff central spine of the coconut frond; and, of course, the single flower behind the ear, of universal appeal. Remember—right side if you're "available," left if "taken."

During the cooler months plumerias drop their leaves, resuming flowering around April. This is normal except for the Singapore plumeria *(P. obtusa)*, a year-round bloomer. Branching low with full, glossy, rich green leaves and large flowers, it is particularly common on O'ahu.

Family: Apocynaceae
Relatives: periwinkle, be-still tree
Other Names: frangipani (British)
Origin: tropical America

The alluring fragrance of a simple white plumeria seems somehow to dispel worries. There are certainly plenty to pick in Hawai'i!

TREE HELIOTROPE
Tournefortia argentea

Family: Boraginaceae
Relatives: forget-me-not, beach heliotrope, *kou*
Other Names: velvetleaf, *tahinu*
Origin: Indo-Pacific coasts

Surrounded by rosettes of large, grayish-green, crispy leaves, the tree heliotrope's flowers and fruits are peculiar but decorative. Try them in low flower arrangements. Its tiny white blossoms, arranged in twisted spiral clusters, are reminiscent of their close relatives, forget-me-nots. As the flowers mature into bunches of small fruits, this curious effect is heightened so that the whole mass resembles numerous greenish octopi snuggled together at the branch tips.

Although distributed throughout the Pacific, this small, hardy, pioneering tree never reached Hawai'i on its own. Since its introduction in the last century it has become perfectly at home around the islands' coasts.

Tree heliotrope is a popular coastal landscaping tree due in part to its resistance to scorching sun, salt, poor soils, and lack of water. Look for its curly "octopi" at beaches such as Ho'okipa State Park, Kahului Harbor, Kā'anapali, Hāna/Hāmoa, Kīhei (Maui); Waikīkī, Kailua, Ala Moana Beach Park (O'ahu); Hilo Harbor (Big Island); Kapa'a and north-coast beaches (Kaua'i).

The tiny, twisted flowers of tree heliotrope mature into masses of writhing green "octopi" nestling within velvety leaves.

Typically a shoreline plant, tree heliotrope here thrives on Hāmoa Beach at Hāna (Maui).

ORANGE FLOWERS OR FRUITS

AFRICAN TULIP TREE
Spathodea campanulata

Year-round clusters of brilliant "tulips" characterize this handsome ornamental, easily recognized even from a distance. Its globes of frilly, cup-shaped flowers, resembling lopsided receptacles of molten steel, protrude boldly from dark glossy foliage.

The introduced African tulip trees are garden escapees and are considered serious pests in some lowland forests. Still, their flaming flashes provide welcome additions to the multi-hued greens of the islands' lush windward coasts and lower mountain slopes: Līhu'e to Hā'ena (Kaua'i), Hāna Highway (Maui), Kāne'ohe to Hale'iwa (O'ahu), and the east and south sections of the Big Island, for example.

They are scattered generously around highways, residential areas, and towns. Look for the yellow-flowered form. Its flowers and leaves produce an attractive series of yellow, fawn, and brown dyes.

Family: Bignoniaceae
Relatives: jacaranda, sausage tree
Origin: tropical Africa

African tulip tree adds a colorful accent to Rainbow Falls, near Hilo (Big Island).

Curved brown buds expand into flattened, frilly "tulips."

HALA
Pandanus spp.

The orange fruitlets of *hala* (pron. hah-lah) or pandanus (p. 57) often litter the ground around coasts, shopping malls, and buildings. These fleshy, squarely triangular seedpods have ripened from pineapplelike fruits that adorn female trees. Don't let anyone fool you that these are "pineapple trees"!

When dry, the fruitlets serve as unique paintbrushes. Fresh ones, carved and strung, create conversation-piece leis. A Hawaiian tradition, still somewhat alive (especially on Oʻahu), is to present a *hala* lei at the beginning of a new phase in someone's life.

Hala fruitlets in three stages of drying. The "paintbrush" end traps air bubbles, assisting in ocean flotation. The mat was woven from *hala* leaves *(lauhala)*.

HIBISCUS
Hibiscus spp.

Orange hibiscus are generally large hybrids that embellish gardens statewide (pp. 29, 37).

KOU
Cordia subcordata

Kou (rhymes with throw), once abundant along coasts and described by missionaries as a "most beautiful tree," suffered a fate in the last century similar to that of elms with Dutch elm disease. Rare for decades, it is now a quite familiar landscaping tree. Orange and crepey, its flowers are only 1 inch across but bud off in clusters practically year-round.

Note the two similar species: Hawaiian *kou (C. subcordata)*, introduced long ago by Polynesians, with shiny leaves; and *kou haole (C. sebestena)*, a more recent introduction, with sandpapery leaves.

In old Hawai'i, *kou* was a much-cherished wood (second only to *koa*), considered "the best" for wooden bowls, trays, and sundry containers. Simply designed, the great *kou* calabashes are now museum specialties. Royal in size (some exceed two feet in diameter), their grain is variegated and glossy.

Family: Boraginaceae
Relatives: forget-me-not, tree helio-
   trope
Origin: Polynesia *(kou)* and West
   Indies *(kou haole)*

Close-up of *kou*.

A precious nineteenth-century *kou* bowl from the Big Island.

How lovely to step out of one's car in an urban parking lot and photograph such an attractive tree! *Kou haole:* Ka'ahumanu Shopping Center (Maui).

MANGO
Mangifera indica

Mango trees, with their full-foliaged crowns of long, dark, pointed leaves, spreading branches, and lavish crops of golden fruits, have long been appreciated as bearers of luscious sweetness and providers of year-round shade.

Cultivated long before the West had thought of orchards and agribusiness, a huge grove was presented to the Buddha (around 600 B.C.) to protect him as he meditated. The first mango seeds brought to Hawai'i (1800–1820) came from India via Mexico, where they had been taken by explorers. The common wild mangoes seen in pastures, large estates, and along rural roads on all islands are descendants of these early types.

Don't let the wild ones ruin your taste for the superior cultivated varieties! Wild fruits are smallish and fibrous, with a taste reminiscent of turpentine. They are best picked green in spring and converted into chutney.

The major garden varieties, Haden (everyone's favorite) and Pirie, belong in a superlative league. Bumper crops occur every two years. Their delectable, creamy, stringless orange pulp is irresistible. Look for them in supermarkets, fruit stands, friends' gardens, or on grassy roadsides. From May to July, carry a penknife and paper towels while traveling.

If you are sensitive to poison ivy/oak/sumac, beware of mangoes. Have someone peel the fruit for you and avoid contact with its leaves and sap.

Family: Anacardiaceae
Relatives: poison ivy, cashew
Origin: India, Burma, Malaysia

Scrumptious Haden mangoes, best in the lowlands from May to July (Wailuku, Maui).

Wild mango leaves are highlighted by a rainbow on the scenic drive five miles north of Hilo (Big Island).

Typical bronzy new leaves of a wild mango tree (Honomanū Bay, Hāna Highway, Maui).

SILK OAK
Grevillea robusta

This showy, golden-flowered tree blooms in a variety of climates and elevations from sea level to 4,000 feet. Reaching 50 to 100 feet tall when mature, it can be seen along highways, as a garden ornamental, or scattered in lowland forests. Introduced around 1900, it is considered one of the twelve best reforestation trees in the islands.

Most noticeable in upcountry Maui and the Kaʻū and Waimea-Kamuela areas (Big Island) from spring to fall, its foliage is clothed with rich orange, fringed blossoms.

Related to Australian "spider bushes," the silk oak's flowers (3–4 inches) resemble an upside-down, stiffish, golden spider with all the legs pointing in one direction, or perhaps a giant golden toothbrush. The large, finely cut leaves have a silvery green sheen on their undersides, especially when young. This sheen, noticeable even from a car, imparts a softness to the leaf and is created by numerous white hairs that help prevent water loss. This is an adaptation to life in dry climates, although the adaptable silk oak will tolerate high rainfall and frosts, too.

Its fine, shiny wood grain, resembling true oak when polished, is esteemed by Australian cabinetmakers. In Hawaiʻi the wood is occasionally used for small carved items such as bracelets.

Family: Proteaceae
Relatives: protea, banksia, macadamia nut, silver tree
Origin: Australia

Silk oak blossom.

Golden floral "spiders" and silvery foliage adorn Kula Highway at 2,500 feet elevation. Māʻalaea Bay and the West Maui Mountains are in the background.

PURPLE FLOWERS

BOUGAINVILLEA
Bougainvillea spectabilis

(See also pp. 19, 37)

GLORYBUSH
Tibouchina urvilleana

A stunning bush with large (3 inches in diameter), bright purple flowers, glorybush was introduced from Brazil around 1910. Later it escaped to the wilds, where it now crowds out native vegetation in a few well-established areas, such as Kalalau Valley Lookout (Kaua'i), Hawaii Volcanoes National Park (Big Island), and on Tantalus and Old Pali Road (O'ahu). Look for glorybush in island gardens at all elevations. Its densely hairy leaves are prominently veined.

Family: Melastomataceae
Relatives: Indian "rhododendron"
Other Names: Lasiandra, tibouchina,
**   princess flower**
Origin: Brazil

A glorybush's profuse, brilliant purple flowers are dazzling.

JACARANDA
Jacaranda mimosaefolia
(= acutifolia)

If there is one predictable seasonal event in Hawai'i, it is the glorious blooming of the brilliant, lavender jacarandas that ushers in spring, as well as tax time and spring vacation! Though jacarandas are sparse around the islands, upcountry Maui and the Waimea-Kamuela area of the Big Island are the prime spots to see this stunning floral display from April to June. Medium-sized to tall trees, jacarandas are best suited to the higher, cooler elevations (2,000–4,000 feet).

On Maui, the drive up to Haleakalā Crater and adjacent towns such as Pukalani, Olinda, and Kula (Routes 37, 377) features hundreds of these lacy-foliaged trees bursting with clusters of tubular bells. Their color is so rich and unusual that one is tempted to pick them.

The grounds of Haleakalā School (Kula, Maui) explode with vibrant color for several months.

STRIPED SUNFLOWER

★ Scrub Jay
★ Plain Titmouse
★ Stellar's Jay
Chestnut-backed Chickadee
House Finch
Purple Finch
White-breasted Nuthatch
House Sparrow
White-crowned Sparrow
Golden-crowned Sparrow

SUPREME

Ideal for birds that feed at an elevated feeder. Supreme is an enticing blend of oil sunflower, sunflower chips and safflower.

DELUXE

For feeding both at the feeder and on the ground, Deluxe, a blend of oil sunflower, millet, sunflower chips and safflower is recommended. Feeder birds select the sunflower and knock the millet to the ground for ground feeders to enjoy.

SELECT

Formulated for ground feeding birds, Select has a high millet content, with some oil sunflower, and is used effectively in a platform feeder or on the ground.

SUNFLOWER CHIPS

The same birds that are attracted to oil and striped sunflower.

WILD BIRDS UNLIMITED CUSTOM BLENDS

Golden-crowned Sparrow
House Sparrow

CRACKED CORN

★ Ducks
★ Pheasants
★ California Quail
Scrub Jay
Dark-eyed Junco
House Sparrow

Wild Birds Unlimited®

71 Brookwood Ave. at 4th St.
Santa Rosa, CA • 576-0861

Available Seeds...
and the Birds They Attract

*Favorite Choice

OIL SUNFLOWER

★ Chestnut-backed Chickadee
★ Black-headed Grosbeak
★ White-crowned Sparrow
★ Plain Titmouse
★ Purple Finch
★ House Finch
★ Stellar's Jay
★ Scrub Jay
★ Red-breasted Nuthatch
★ White-breasted Nuthatch
Pine Siskin
Dark-eyed Junco
Song Sparrow
Golden-crowned Sparrow
Mourning Dove
House Sparrow

WHITE MILLET

★ Golden-crowned Sparrow
★ Mourning Dove
★ Dark-eyed Junco
★ California Quail
★ Rufous-sided Towhee
★ California Towhee
★ House Sparrow

NIGER-THISTLE

★ American Goldfinch
★ Lesser Goldfinch
★ Pine Siskin
House Finch
Mourning Dove
Dark-eyed Junco
Purple Finch

SAFFLOWER

(Squirrels and blackbirds avoid)
Chestnut-backed Chickadee
Mourning Dove
House Finch
Stellar's Jay
Scrub Jay
White-breasted Nuthatch
House Sparrow
Plain Titmouse

PEANUTS

★ Chestnut-backed Chickadee
★ Red-breasted Nuthatch
★ White-breasted Nuthatch
★ Plain Titmouse
★ Woodpeckers
★ Jays

Unfortunately, both the feathery leaves and the flowers droop rapidly. Individual blossoms, however, make beautiful, unique leis. Thread the needle *across* the flower end rather than *through* it from one end to the other. Try them alone or mixed with fuchsias. If misted lightly and refrigerated, the lei lasts overnight.

Family: Bignoniaceae
Relatives: African tulip tree, tecoma
Origin: Argentina, Bolivia

JAVA PLUM
Eugenia cuminii

Although abundant in the lowlands and lower foothills of Hawai'i, Java plum is a somewhat nondescript tree that may not attract your attention until you end up scrubbing dark, persistent stains from your car, tent, or clothes. This tree's purplish-black fruits, similar in size and shape to olives, are borne in numerous dangling clusters during the fall, when they drop, squashing their tender skins and staining everything below them.

Java plums *are* edible, but they tend to be a little astringent (like underripe persimmons) and not particularly sweet. I enjoy them as hiking snacks. Some local families gather them to make jelly, but this is a time-consuming project because by the time the skins and large seed are strained out, there's not much pulp left.

The leaves of this medium-sized tree are variable but generally elliptical (3 to 8 inches long). They tend to hang vertically like eucalyptus foliage.

For obvious reasons, Java plum is not

Clusters of purplish-black berries drop in the fall.

suitable for commercial or private landscaping in confined areas, especially parking lots! Once you develop an eye for them, you'll spot them on practically every drive in rural areas, particularly along the windward coasts of all major islands. Locations near waterfalls and streams are always good, for example, Hālawa Valley (Moloka'i), Wailua Falls (Kaua'i), 'Iao Valley and Kīpahulu (Maui), and Wahiawā-Waimea area (O'ahu).

Family: Myrtaceae
Relatives: apple, guava
Other Names: jambolan plum
Origin: Southeast Asia

Sunshine after a downpour highlights Hīpuapua Falls, which plummets into Hālawa Valley, Moloka'i, amidst canopies of monkeypod, *kukui*, and roadside Java plum trees.

ORCHID TREE
Bauhinia spp.

These pleasantly configured trees, bearing masses of dainty, orchidlike flowers bursting open amid butterfly-shaped leaves, are sparkles of beauty in the lowlands of Hawai'i. These showpieces are scattered around gardens and streets on all islands: Lahaina-Kā'anapali, Kahului (Maui); Līhu'e (Kaua'i);

On closer examination, one can see that orchid tree blossoms are not true orchids, but only superficially resemble them.

Hilo, Kona (Big Island); Honolulu and Kāneʻohe-Kailua (Oʻahu).

Their elegant blossoms, 3 inches in diameter, are pinkish-mauve, purple, or white. Flowering begins in spring and continues for several months. Orchid trees, which reach 20 to 30 feet high, love sunshine and low elevations. They are unrelated to true orchids. (See also p. 24.)

Family: Leguminosae
Relatives: sweet pea, monkeypod, shower trees
Other Names: pink bauhinia, St. Thomas tree, butterfly tree
Origin: New and Old World tropics

Orchid trees flank ʻAʻala Street near downtown Honolulu (Oʻahu).

GREEN FRUITS

AVOCADO
Persea americana

Everyone knows these green (also purple or brown), pear-shaped fruits that dangle from medium-sized trees. In Hawai'i, several varieties provide a year-round supply; most are available from spring to summer. Conspicuous in both lowland and upland gardens and occasionally in the wild, avocados are well-established favorites of Hawai'i homeowners.

This has not always been so. When avocados were introduced to the islands in the 1820s, the first residents were disenchanted with this "fabulous new fruit." Many decades later, after the establishment of superior, grafted varieties, its subtly delicious qualities became appreciated. Today practically every restaurant offers some type of delicacy that includes avocados. (Most commercially available ones are Fuertes, imports from California: that is why avocados are more expensive in Hawai'i than in California!)

The name "avocado" reflects its native homeland, tropical America. The Aztec *ahucatl* was converted by Spanish settlers into *aguacate*, then later changed to *avocado* by the British. The British also called them "alligator pears," presumably because of their pearlike shape and rough, leathery skin. Even today, old-timers in Hawai'i prefer the names "winter pear" or just plain "pear." If a friend offers you some "pears," don't be surprised to discover a bag of avocados!

Family: Lauraceae
Relatives: cinnamon, bay, camphor
Other Names: alligator pear, "pear"
Origin: tropical America

Avocado trees are a familiar sight around homes in Hawai'i. (Photo by Riki Saito)

Many delectable varieties of avocado are grown in Hawai'i, mostly in home gardens. (Photo by Riki Saito)

BREADFRUIT
Artocarpus altilis

With coconut palms and *hala* trees, breadfruit ranks as one of the world's great trees in terms of artistry, utility, and cultural associations. Breadfruit has long symbolized the exuberant tropics and its attendant way of life.

In Hawaiian mythology, breadfruit originated from the magical transmutation of the great god Kū. During a devastating famine, Kū informed his wife that during the night his body would change into a tree trunk and branches, his hands into leaves, his head into

Light filters through breadfruit leaves along the route to Moaʻula Falls (Hālawa Valley, Molokaʻi).

Globular fruits, sometimes as large as one's head, adorn this Polynesian-introduced tropical beauty, breadfruit.

fruit, and his tongue into the fruit's "heart" to save his people.

Breadfruit's 1- to 3-foot-long, dark, glossy leaves with deeply indented lobes resemble huge leathery hands. Its familiar fruits (up to several pounds) are formed by the coalition of hundreds of individual flowers, much like a pineapple. Adorning well-established gardens (especially in rural areas or in Hawaiian communities), breadfruit particularly abounds in Keʻanae, Hāna, Kīpahulu (Maui); Hālawa Valley (Molokaʻi); Hanalei to Hāʻena (Kauaʻi); Hilo to Puna (Big Island); and Mānoa Valley and the north shore of Oʻahu.

Try this: sauté thin slices of partly ripe fruit in butter and garlic. It's delicious!

Family: Moraceae
Relatives: jakfruit, figs, mulberry, banyan
Other Names: *ʻulu*
Origin: Pacific islands

FALSE KAMANI
Terminalia catappa

Abundant throughout the island lowlands, false kamanis line almost every
beach and rocky foreshore, flank roads,
speckle pastures, and dress up hotels,
condos, fast-food restaurants, airports,
and city parks. Their tiered, wide-
spreading, horizontal branches bear
rosettes of large, spoon-shaped leaves.
Within these rosettes, 6-inch spikes of
tiny white flowers appear, soon enlarg-
ing to form almond-shaped, green
fruits. If you care to expend the time
and energy with a penknife, each con-
tains a tasty "almond."

Although it is a warm-climate evergreen, continuously shedding leaves,
the false kamani differs from the norm

False kamani flourishes especially on
windward shorelines, near Hāna (Maui).

Abundant along coasts, false kamani is seen
here framing a view of Keʻanae (Maui).

This is the closest Hawai'i comes to Vermont's fall colors!

in that its dying leaves, while still intact, turn yellow, red, orange, and brown, imparting an early autumn character to the tree and ground beneath it.

Although frequently encountered, note them especially embellishing beaches of windward O'ahu and Kaua'i, Hilo Harbor (Big Island), and Hāna Bay (Maui).

Family: Combretaceae
Other Names: tropical, West Indian, or country almond; *kamani haole; kamani* (confusing because of true kamani, an unrelated tree)
Origin: Southeast Asia

Long, narrow flower spikes and green almond-shaped seedpods appear year-round on false kamani. Try the tasty "almond" inside the thick nut.

HALA
Pandanus tectorius

Evolutionarily one of the world's most ancient plants (over 250 million years old), a nature spirit and progenitor of the human race in Hawaiian mythology, the picturesque *hala* has been, and continues to be, utilized and loved by Pacific peoples. Its uses are legion: mats, woven items, housing, food, ornaments, pillows, fishing implements, religion, and medicine. Interestingly, the tips of actively growing aerial roots were known to contain healing powers; we know today that rapidly growing tissues (e.g., sprouted grains) are plentifully endowed with

"Prop" or "stilt" roots of *hala* help the soft wood of its trunk withstand strong coastal winds.

Winter storm surf at Ho'okipa Beach lends a wild Pacific ambience to the north coast of Maui, minutes from Kahului airport.

potent chemicals and life-giving energy conducive to health.

Primarily a coastal tree, its elongated, spirally tufted leaves and prop roots make *hala* unmistakable. Look for it on nearly every beach in Hawaii (except, curiously, Waikīkī), around cities (Ala Moana Park, libraries, hotels, etc.), and along coastal highways, particularly in wet, windward areas (e.g., Hāna Highway to Kīpahulu, Maui; windward coast, Oʻahu; Luma-

The fruit of *hala*, only borne on female trees, resemble pineapples, but don't let anyone fool you! The people of old Hawaiʻi did not eat these fruits, but in Micronesia they are still popular as sweetish snacks.

Hala frames a view of Kēʻē Beach (Kalalau Trail, Kauaʻi).

ha'i and other north-coast beaches, Kaua'i).

Lauhala (literally "leaf of the *hala*"), when de-spined and woven, is used for the well-known *lauhala* mats. Their naturally lustrous, "plastic" finish, impervious to dirt, lends an informal tropical flavor to many island homes. All mats today are imported from the South Pacific. Authentic Hawaiian mats still exist in old Hawaiian churches (especially on the Big Island and Maui) and as treasures at the Bishop Museum.

Children are frequently attracted to the orange fruitlets that have fallen from the pineapplelike fruits of *hala* (p. 42).

Family: Pandanaceae
Relatives: *'ie'ie* vine
**Other Names: pandanus, screwpine,
    *pū hala***
Origin: Polynesia

Pollen from male flowers of *hala*, either alone or suspended in coconut oil, was an aphrodisiac used in old Hawai'i by young girls while attempting to attract boyfriends.

Ala Moana Shopping Center seen through *hala* (Ala Moana Park, Honolulu).

Spiral tufts of *hala* always enhance the view around lower mountain slopes and lowlands (Waikamoi Ridge Trail, Maui).

JAKFRUIT
Artocarpus heterophyllus

Family: Moraceae (see bread-fruit, p. 53)

A close relative of breadfruit, jakfruit is identified by its huge, knobbed, edible fruit. One of the world's most gigantic fruits, healthy ones may weigh 40 pounds and attain 3 feet in length.

The jakfruit bears enormous fruit (though less tasty than breadfruit) directly from its trunk (Keʻanae Arboretum, Hāna Highway, Maui).

INCONSPICUOUS FLOWERS OR FRUITS

BANYANS
Ficus spp.

The banyan's curious aggregation of dangling aerial roots and multiple trunks makes it unmistakable. Children love to climb the intertwining trunks (some trees are over 100 years old), clamber across spreading branches, and swing, Tarzan-style, from the twisted masses of aerial roots.

Banyans exude character. Is this due to the unique shape of each individual? Their association with shady, cool places? Their rich mythology? Their venerable age, complete with long "beards" and extra "legs"? Their attraction of an abundance of bird and

Slanting flanges of the Chinese banyan reach skyward at Pau Hāna Inn (Kaunakakai, Moloka'i).

A restful spot for a quiet moment in Honolulu (Thomas Square, Ward Avenue). The plant's name is derived from ancient Hindu merchants, banyans, who spread their wares beneath these shady trees.

insect life within their expanses? Or a combination of all?

Indian *(F. benghalensis)* and Chinese *(F. microcarpa)* banyans are common in Hawai'i, especially in Honolulu. Note that the Chinese species has fewer auxiliary trunks and pendant roots, and the trunk has an obliquely ribbed appearance.

Notable trees are at 'Iolani Palace (in the late nineteenth century, carriages drove between the two original trees bringing guests to visit King Kalākaua) and Thomas Square (encircling the fountain between the Academy of Arts and Blaisdell Center). Many grace Waikīkī in hotel courtyards, Kapi'olani Park, along the beachfront (near Waikīkī Aquarium), and in the International Market Place. On the neighbor islands, two famous spots are in Lahaina, Maui (opposite the Pioneer Inn, where one tree covers almost an acre) and beautiful Banyan Drive, Hilo (Big Island).

See p. 66 for other types of fig trees.

Family: Moraceae
Relatives: mulberry; *wauke* (paper mulberry), from which tapa is made
Origin: warm regions worldwide

Late-afternoon light highlights the aerial roots and shiny leaves of an Indian banyan. Listen for myna birds at this time of day.

COOK PINE
Araucaria columnaris

Lacking native pines, island residents have adopted this prickly but handsome "pine" as their Christmas tree. Native to New Caledonia and the Isle of Pines, Cook pine seeds first broke Hawaiian soil on Lāna'i in the 1870s. Some of the original trees arc still alive, towering above Lāna'i City. One giant on the Big Island was 109 feet tall when last measured.

Though Cook pines line city and rural byways on every island, Lāna'i is the best placc to experience their grandeur. Note them as you fly into Lāna'i and Moloka'i airports.

Moist regions encourage the richest growth and greatest symmetry. Ha'ikū and Kokomo (Maui) are good areas for Christmas tree farms. The symmetrical perfection of young trees makes them appear almost artificial. Their stiff leaves, very sharp when young, are not arranged in tufts like pine needles; they emerge singly from the branches, overlapping one another as the tree matures. Besides "Hawaiian Christmas tree," another local name is "star pine." Each tier of several branches radiates from a central point, resembling a flat, green, prickly star.

For more than a century, this tree in Hawai'i has been confused with the closely related Norfolk Island pine *(Araucaria heterophylla)*. In fact, most of the trees popularly called Norfolk Island pines in Hawai'i are actually Cook pines, and these are the source of seeds, young Christmas trees, and lumber that is exported to the U.S. mainland.

Family: Araucariaceae
Relatives: monkey puzzle tree, Australian kauri
Other Names: star pine, Hawaiian Christmas tree, columnar araucaria
Origin: New Caledonia and Isle of Pines

Close-up of the Cook pine's growing tip, showing the single, sharp needles emerging from both trunk and branches.

A row of Cook pines edges a Christmas tree farm (Kokomo, Maui).

EUCALYPTUS
Eucalyptus spp.

Don't even begin to sort out all 75-odd species of eucalyptus in Hawai'i! There are too many look-alikes. A few are easy. Swamp mahogany *(E. robusta)*, with deeply furrowed bark, is commonly planted by the Division of Forestry for soil stabilization and its valuable, rich-grained wood, which is so hard that nail holes must be predrilled. Unfortunately, its roots are shallow, thus majestic stands can be reduced by high winds to masses of jumbled 100-foot logs practically overnight.

A beautiful, parklike tunnel of swamp mahogany lines the route to Kōloa and Po'ipū (Kaua'i). Extensive stands have been planted along the Hāna Highway (Maui) and the Hāmākua Coast (Big Island).

Blue gums *(E. globulus)* possess decidedly bluish, fragrant young foliage. Entire groves, especially after rains, have a medicinal smell. What a marvelous aroma, nostalgic to both Australians and Californians! Several tracts flank the zigzag road up to Haleakalā Crater (Maui).

The arresting Mindanao gum *(E. deglupta)* has a smooth trunk "painted" in shades of lime, green, blue, lavender, red, orange, gray, and indigo, which dance iridescently in the sunlight. The first seed was planted at

Lyon Arboretum (O'ahu) in 1939. The tree is now 90 feet tall and still growing.

Though uncommon, Mindanao gum is found along the Hāna Highway (Maui) near Waikamoi bamboo forest and at Ke'anae Arboretum.

Swamp mahogany, a prime reforestation tree, is a common sight along neighbor island roads. It often pairs with the native *uluhe* fern, as here along the Hāna Highway (Maui).

Gorgeous yellow light, reminiscent of the high latitudes, shines on eucalyptus and pastures of 'Ulupalakua Ranch (Maui).

Uncommon but unmistakable, the Mindanao gum's trunk dances with color in the sunlight (Keʻanae Arboretum, Maui).

Family: Myrtaceae
Relatives: ʻōhiʻa, guava
Other Names: gum trees
Origin: Australia; Mindanao gum is unusual, as it comes from the Philippine Islands

Tall, majestic stands of swamp mahogany are especially evident on the Hāmākua coast, north of Hilo (Big Island).

Eucalyptus trees have been planted extensively by the State Division of Forestry and private landowners. At elevations above 4,000 feet they are often shrouded in mists, such as this blue gum stand along the road to Haleakalā Crater (Maui).

The native, endangered Hawaiian hawk, or ʻio (Buteo solitarius), found only on the Big Island, sits in a blue gum tree not far from Hilo. (Photo by David Boynton)

FIG TREES
Ficus spp.

In addition to banyans, landscaping in Hawai'i includes numerous other figs. Of approximately 800 species native to warm regions of the world, over 100 have been introduced to the islands. Once you develop an eye for them, you'll spot them frequently, even as large potted plants in unlikely spots such as the dentist's office.

Many have small, glossy, pointed leaves, for example, weeping fig *(F. benjamina)*. Popular is the India rubber tree *(F. elastica)*, whose long, glossy leaves are at first enclosed in a pointed pink sheath. India rubber trees line the drive into the Kā'anapali hotel complex (Maui). This particular species is the one from which rubber was originally made, and it is also often used as

India rubber tree is a popular ornamental around hotels, in commercially landscaped areas, and in botanic gardens.

Weeping figs are common ornamentals, generally in parks (Thomas Square, Honolulu) but also as potted plants in offices.

a potted plant, in Hawai'i and on the U.S. mainland.

Ala Moana Park (Honolulu) is home to several species of figs, which bear small orange, red, or brownish fruits. Break one apart; you'll recognize it immediately as a member of the fig family.

In Hawai'i, not all fig trees develop fruits, as the wasps necessary to pollinate them are not present. Fruit-eating birds such as doves and bulbuls take advantage of the bounteous crops of fruit.

Family: Moraceae
Relatives: mulberry, *wauke* (paper mulberry or tapa plant), banyan
Origin: warm regions worldwide

Though not as large as edible figs, fruits from the numerous species of ornamental figs are similar botanically. In their native countries, these are often eaten by bats; in Hawai'i, birds reap the bounty almost exclusively. Shown is *F. macrophylla*.

IRONWOOD
Casuarina equisetifolia

The shaggy, long-needled, drooping "pines" flanking island shorelines are not pines at all but Australian ironwoods. Hawai'i has no native pines, but because of the ironwood's early introduction and its superficial resemblance to pines, Hawaiians named the species *paina*. The slender "needles" that wave in the breeze are actually pendant, jointed stems, and the spiky "cones" (watch out if you have bare feet) have a totally different make-up from regular pine cones.

Carried over vast stretches of the Pacific by Polynesian voyagers (but not to Hawai'i), ironwoods are rich in cultural lore. Tahitians believe they sprang from the bodies of fallen warriors, whose blood turned into red sap and hair into stringy "leaves." Its ironlike wood was carved into weapons, which reputedly possessed *mana* (supernatural powers).

Ironwood's association with war became so strong that even its Polynesian name, *toa*, became synonymous with "warrior" and "bravery." Their

Abundant along coastlines, ironwood here frames Hanalei Bay (north coast, Kaua'i). (Photo by Cameron Kepler)

roots were purposely bent and allowed to continue growing, eventually to become large, one-piece shark hooks. The first traders in Hawai'i were surprised to find that the nails they traded were subsequently bent and partly buried. Ironwood was the hardest sub-

stance known to island natives and, if iron nails were harder, then maybe they might grow into good fish-hooks too!

The several species of ironwoods (casuarinas) are rather drab but useful in arresting coastal erosion. A hardy product of millions of years of evolution, ironwoods can survive under harsh, salty, dry, and windy conditions, braving storms and burning sun with equal stalwartness.

Family: Casuarinaceae
Other Names: common casuarina, she-oak, Australian pine, *paina*
Origin: Australia

Slender, drooping ironwood stems mimic pine needles on the south coast of Moloka'i.

KIAWE
Prosopis pallida

Though not a dazzling beauty, *kiawe* covers such vast acreage that it deserves mention. Your encounters with it may be unusual: a *kiawe*-broiled steak, *kiawe* honey, or a sharp pain as its long thorns pierce your bare feet or shoes at the beach. They often puncture tires!

Typical of dry, leeward areas, the appearance of *kiawe* varies depending on local climate and geographic condi-

Kiawe covers vast areas of pasture and wastelands in Hawai'i. Watch out for their fallen spines!

During dry spells, hillslopes of *kiawe* appear drab, but when rain resumes they spring forth anew (southern mountains, Moloka'i).

tions. When well watered or shaded, its tiny leaves and long, slender branches (*kiawe* means swaying) are quite lush. More often, though, rolling mauve-gray expanses of it look half dead.

Today's millions of trees originated from a single seed planted in Honolulu by a Catholic priest in 1828. Now it provides protein-rich fodder, fuel, lumber, and charcoal, and it is used for reforestation on the barren wastelands of Kaho'olawe. *Kiawe* abounds along shores and on uninhabited lands, pasturelands, and lower foothills: Pearl Harbor environs (O'ahu), Kīhei, Mā'alaea, Lahaina (Maui), and the south coasts of Moloka'i and Kaua'i.

Family: Leguminosae
Relatives: *koa haole*, *koa*, mesquite
Origin: Peru

Closely related *koa haole (Leucaena leucocephala)*, also abundant in wastelands, has pompon flowers, instead of the long yellowish spikes typical of *kiawe*, and no spines.

KOA
Acacia koa

The fresh golden pollen of *koa* pompon flowers lends a subtle, sweet fragrance to spring.

Koa. The name brings to mind tall native forests of majestic trees from which durable canoes, heavy surfboards, and precious calabashes were fashioned. In ancient Hawai'i it symbolized "health, wealth, and well-being."

Originally covering vast expanses of mountain forests (1,000–6,000 feet elevation), *koa* trees were early sacrificed for ranchlands. Today, in the limited upland areas where they still exist, they lend a distinctly Hawaiian flavor.

Accessible *koa* trees are at the Waimea Canyon rim and Kōke'e region (Kaua'i); forests *mauka* of Kona, and the Strip Road in Hawaii Volcanoes National Park (Big Island); and Hāna Highway near Pua'aka'a State Park (Maui). Hikers can also encounter them in Hakalau Preserve and Kīlauea Forest Reserve (Big Island), Waikamoi

A remnant stand of native *koa*, an extra treat after hiking through Haleakalā Crater and down Kaupō Gap (Maui). (Photo by John Carothers)

Preserve and Kaupō Gap (Maui), and on Tantalus–Round Top (Oʻahu).

Koa floors, ukuleles, tables, bowls, and even picture frames spell luxury. The wood grain is close, sometimes "curly," and variegated with rich reds and creams.

Although *koa* wood is gorgeous, one should be aware that, if conservationists had more power, logging of remaining *koa* forests would halt immediately. Natural supplies will not last much longer and *koa* grown on plantations does not easily form tall, straight trees of commercial value.

I include *koa* here because it is one of the islands' most esteemed natural resources. Not to have heard of *koa*, rich in beauty and steeped in island tradition, is akin to never having heard of *mahimahi* or saimin—such ignorance stamps you as a true *malihini* (newcomer)!

Family: Leguminosae
Relatives: *koa haole*, peas, shower trees
Origin: Hawaiian Islands

Peeking out through *koa* leaves is the Japanese white-eye or mejiro *(Zosterops japonicus)*.

KUKUI
Aleurites moluccana

Offering us a wealth of esthetic beauty and cultural heritage, this "maple"-leaved Polynesian introduction, whose pale green billows of foliage nestle in forested gullies on every island, is the state tree of Hawaiʻi. The "lei of Molokaʻi" is fashioned by intertwining its leaves.

Though infrequent in gardens and landscaping (its discarded leaves and nuts are messy), *kukui* trees are abundant in moist, rural lowlands and on lower mountain slopes, especially on neighbor islands, for example, ʻĪao Valley, Hāna Highway (Maui); north coastal road (Kauaʻi); roads north, south, and west of Hilo (Big Island); and the east-coast road of Molokaʻi.

Abundant in forested areas, *kukui* is always recognizable by its very pale foliage (Waikolu Valley, Molokaʻi). (Photo by Cameron Kepler)

On closer examination, *kukui* leaves resemble those of maple trees.

Present in Hawai'i since A.D. 400 *kukui* has adapted well to the natural environments. Its greenish-white clusters of small flowers are present year-round. In old Hawai'i, the green walnutlike nuts provided medicines, dyes, surfboard stains, and a linseedlike oil. *Kukui* nuts should not be eaten because the uncooked nut is a drastic purge.

"Shish kebabs" of dried *kukui* nuts and stone mortars of expressed oil were the only source of light until foreigners brought matches and taught Hawaiians how to make a flame from beef tallow. Early missionaries called it the "candlenut" tree.

Family: Euphorbiaceae
Relatives: poinsettia, croton
Other Names: candlenut
Origin: Asia, Pacific islands

MONEY TREE
Pleomele marginata

Resembling California's joshua trees, money trees, with their tufted clumps of narrow, pink-edged leaves on long stalks, are popular ornamentals. First planted in the 1920s on the grounds of the old Bishop Bank in Hilo, these plants immediately became associated with banks and the curious local name "money tree" has stayed with us.

Like its relative *ti* (p. 80), the long stalks of the money tree can be radically pruned if the tree becomes lanky (use the pruned tufts for flower arranging). New sprouts appear quickly.

A charming cultivar is the Japanese 'tricolor,' whose leaves sport bright pink, green, and cream vertical stripes. Fuller and more graceful than its relative above, 'tricolor' is so common now in nurseries and tropical gardens (e.g., Helani Gardens, Hāna, Maui) that it is exported as tropical foliage accompanying heliconias and gingers.

The charming cultivar 'tricolor' was introduced from Japan in 1969.

Family: Liliaceae
Relatives: agave, joshua tree, lily
Other Names: Madagascar dragon tree
Origin: Madagascar

Money trees are popular ornamentals around towns and cities on all islands (Honolulu).

PALMS
Family Palmae

With tall trunks and gracefully waving fronds, palms epitomize the tropics. From this huge family of approximately 3,000 species worldwide, almost 800 species have been introduced into Hawai'i. About 30 species are reasonably common.

The following pages depict the palms most likely to be encountered and identified by the average traveler or resident. Additional collections may be enjoyed at Foster Botanic Garden (Honolulu), which specializes in palms; Waimea and Lyon arboretums; Wahiawā Botanic Garden; and Ho'omaluhia (O'ahu), and National Tropical Botanical Garden (Lāwa'i, Kaua'i).

Coconut and Alexandra palms beautify the scenic drive north of Hilo (Big Island).

ALEXANDRA PALM
Archontophoenix alexandrae

I include this beautiful, erect, Australian palm because of its preponderance on the Big Island. Thousands embellish the lush roadsides, river valleys, pastures, edges of cane fields, and residential areas of the wet, windward side.

The foot-long, creamy flower cluster arises below the fronds where the green cylinder meets the trunk. Look for them en route to Hawaii Volcanoes National Park from Hilo.

A clump of Alexandra palms adds charm to Rainbow Falls (Big Island).

CHINESE FAN PALM
Livistona chinensis

The leaves of this widely planted palm (usually growing singly or in twos) project stiffly outward then droop, imparting a curled, stringy appearance to the "fan."

Other fan palms, imported from all over the world, include the extremely stiff, blue latan palm *(Latania loddigesii)* and *loulu* (*Pritchardia* spp.), some of which are native to the islands.

Chinese fan palms add a delightfully tropical flavor to island landscaping.

COCONUT PALM
Cocos nucifera

This proverbial "feather duster" has enticed millions of adventurers, tourists, writers, artists, surfers, and others to tropical shores. A "gift of life" to islanders Pacific-wide, it was originally brought to Hawai'i by adventurous Polynesians.

Even though the nuts can withstand four months of floating and still germinate, coconuts never reached Hawai'i unaided. This was due to the islands' extreme isolation and the nature of the surrounding ocean currents. Ancient Pacific uses included matting, thatching, food, syrup, toys, cordage, body oil, medicines, and shelter, while mod-

Though loaded with hundreds of yellow flowers on each floral branch, only a fraction of them mature into coconuts.

In this age of safety consciousness, most ornamental coconut palms in Hawai'i are regularly trimmed. Not so this veteran grove near Kaunakakai, Moloka'i. (The Samoans claim that coconuts don't fall on the heads of good people anyway!)

ern uses include soap, margarine, cosmetics, "coconut hats," Christmas decorations, and, of paramount importance, land beautification. You are greeted by waving coconut palms from the moment your plane banks to land in Honolulu.

Strewn around city and country on every island (up to about 2,000 feet elevation), these captivating palms grace beaches, highways, gardens, hotels, lush lowland valleys, and pastures. Particularly attractive groves are at Coco Palms Resort (Kaua'i) and Kaunakakai (Moloka'i).

The mature palms you see around most hotels, banks, and other public buildings were transplanted to form "instant landscaping." The aluminum trunk guards prevent rats from climbing up and building nests.

Split a green-brown nut open with a hatchet and enjoy its tasty, nutritious "meat" and refreshing "coconut water." Contrary to popular opinion, "coconut milk" is *not* the liquid found naturally inside the coconut, but is a rich, creamy white liquid made from grated "meat" steeped in hot water then strained. It is used in piña coladas, along with pineapple juice and rum.

Coconut palms are used extensively in island landscaping and can be transplanted when fully mature. Here they accent the immaculate gardens of Wailea 'Ekāhi (Maui).

Muted colors silhouetting coastal coconut palms at Lahaina epitomize the tranquility of a tropical evening.

Many people's idea of "perfect living" is a little house in Hāna dwarfed by bounteous coconut palms.

DATE PALM
Phoenix dactylifera

Steeped in tradition, not from Polynesia but from arid Africa and the Near East, date palms are sprinkled around Hawai'i, thriving particularly in dry areas, such as Kanahā Pond, Lahaina, Maui.

Though capable of producing up to 3,000 pounds of fruit annually, the fruit is of poor quality and most of it is lost to greedy mynas, other fruit-eating birds, and rats.

Note the full circular crown with "skirt" of dried fronds.

Early morning reflections of date palms at Kanahā Pond (Maui).

Beautiful afternoon light accentuates date palms near the former settlement for Hansen's disease patients on Kalaupapa Peninsula (Moloka'i).

GOLDEN-FRUITED PALM
Chrysalidocarpus lutescens

Abundantly used in Hawaiian landscaping, this beautiful palm is easily recognized by its circular clumps of slender, bamboolike trunks bearing gracefully arching fronds with pointed leaflets.

When fruiting, the berries are golden. Clustered around the bases of the larger trunks (up to 20 feet high) are offshoots of various sizes. Golden-fruited palms make elegant centerpieces for spacious lawns; dress up residences, churches, and office buildings; and form attractive hedges.

Where space is limited they grow well in large pots, indoors or outdoors. (It is sold as the "areca" palm in nurseries.) The similarly clustered Macarthur palm *(Ptychosperma macarthuri)* possesses blunt-ended leaflets and red berries.

A golden-fruited palm at Maria Lanakila Church, Lahaina (Maui).

MANILA PALM
Veitchia merrillii

A short, formal, tidy-looking palm from the Philippines, the Manila palm is one of the islands' most common landscaping palms. It is also popular in Florida.

Look for its firmly arching leaves and clusters of bright red fruits (especially during fall and winter) along city roadsides and around banks, hotels, and office buildings.

Bright December fruits of the Manila palm frame the serene Buddha at Lahaina Jodo Mission (Maui).

RHAPIS PALM
Rhapis excelsa

Shrubby clumps of this shiny-leaved dwarf palm (reminiscent of Florida palmettos) are popular in gardens, on patios, in hotel and restaurant entranceways, and around banks; they occur occasionally in the wild. Native to China and Japan, this palm's numerous, bamboolike stems rarely exceed 6 or 7 feet in height.

Rhapis palms amid lush, jungly undergrowth ('Akaka Falls Trail, Big Island).

ROYAL PALM
Roystonea regia

Stately palms (up to 70 feet high) with feathery crowns, these are distinguished from coconut palms by pale, banded, smooth gray trunks; three-dimensional leaves; a vertical "spike" (unopened leaf sheath) emerging from the top; a smooth green cylinder of leaf bases looking like a continuation of the trunk; and a greatly branched flower cluster arising from the point where the smooth green cylinder and trunk meet.

Royal palms are always completely upright and occur in planted situations away from the ocean, generally in double rows flanking driveways. Native to Cuba, the first seeds were planted on O'ahu in 1850.

Notable avenues lined with royal palms are at Punahou School (Honolulu), Lahainaluna School (Maui), and Royal Palm Drive, Wahiawā (central O'ahu).

Elegant royal palms line an avenue at the prestigious, missionary-founded Punahou School in Honolulu.

TI
Cordyline fruticosa

Family: Agavaceae
Relatives: dracaenas, lilies
Other Names: *kī*
Origin: tropical Asia, Pacific islands

A distinctive large-leaved, rosetted shrub, ti is cloaked in Pacific folklore. In the days before plastic bags and refrigeration, *ti*'s multitudinous uses included sandals, raincoats, medicines, fishing accessories, plates, temporary thatching, toboggans, sweet baked roots, an alcoholic "beer," cooking and storage wrappers, and fly whisks. If you have a headache, try an old remedy: wet a *ti* leaf and let it refresh your forehead. *Ti*'s shiny, waxy leaves are commonly 2 feet long and 5 inches wide.

They still have many uses. One traditional use is for *laulau*, which can be enjoyed at a Hawaiian feast *(lū'au)* or backyard party. To make *laulau*, pieces of meat or fish and taro leaves are wrapped in *ti* leaves and cooked slowly in their own juices (like cornhusk tamales). Try making a bow from a single leaf and then add a flower adornment to dress up party tables.

Ti plants and its numerous cultivars abound in Hawai'i: in residential or botanic gardens, in lush wild vegetation, and around condos and hotels. Planted to the right of one's front door, *ti* reputedly wards off evil spirits. I cannot guarantee its efficacy, but our front entranceway sports a *ti* on the right and heavenly bamboo (Japanese good-luck plant) on the left, just in case!

A graceful *ti* branch frames 'Akaka Falls (Big Island). The pale trees below are cecropias from tropical America.

Wide and shiny, *ti* leaves are abundant along Hāna Highway (Maui).

TRAVELER'S TREE
Ravenala madagascariensis

A close relative of the giant bird of paradise (which its flowers resemble), this unusual tree is unmistakable. A huge, two-dimensional fan reaching 40 feet high, its constituent leaf bases overlap, forming an attractive "woven" pattern. Unless trimmed frequently (using ladders), the tree becomes most untidy.

Some vow that under natural conditions the traveler's tree "fan" orients north and south, providing a compass direction for the lost traveler. Others claim that thirsty voyagers can quench their thirst from the ample water held between the leaf bases. Judging by the tree's height and its tendency to collect large amounts of debris, plus the large numbers of mosquito larvae and other aquatic life that live quite happily within this water supply, one might conclude that drinkable water could better be found elsewhere!

Traveler's trees thrive in moist, humid, shady environments and can be seen in Foster Botanic Garden (Honolulu), Royal Hawaiian Shopping Center (Waikīkī), National Tropical Botanical

Garden (Kaua'i), Hotel Hāna Maui and Helani Gardens (Maui), and around Hilo (Big Island). Although often called "traveler's palm," it is not related to true palms.

Family: Musaceae
Relatives: bird of paradise, heliconia, banana
Other Names: traveler's palm
Origin: Madagascar

Traveler's tree: what a wonderfully neat arrangement of leaf bases! The rest of the leaf looks like a banana frond.

Originally from Madagascar, this immaculately tended traveler's tree lends tropical elegance to a condominium in Wailea (Maui).

TREE FERNS (*HĀPU'U*)

Cibotium spp.

If you visit the Big Island, on no account miss a walk through the beautiful tree fern forests of Hawaii Volcanoes National Park. Thurston Lava Tube is excellent. Embowering you in apple-green lucency are tall, lacy fronds, exquisite in color and symmetry. From the center of each stately tree fern arise furry stems, proudly crowned with woolly, unfurling fiddleheads that bear a striking resemblance to the scrollheads of orchestral double basses.

Framed in lacy tree ferns, a Big Island waterfall plunges toward Hilo to become drinking and bath water (Ho'okelekele Stream, 1,600 feet elevation).

Fit for a symphony, this hairy fiddlehead *(Cibotium chamissoi)* unfurls deep in a pristine forest on Moloka'i.

Tree ferns *(Cibotium hawaiense)* are common in Hawaii Volcanoes National Park (Big Island) and as garden ornamentals throughout the state.

Part of the natural forest understory, tree ferns (six native species) instill a magic to forest verdure. The silky fluff protecting young fronds, called *pulu*, was used by early Hawaiians for embalming the dead. Later, in the nineteenth century, it was popular (even exported) for stuffing pillows and quilts. The airiness of *pulu*, unfortunately, was only temporary—pillows soon degenerated into sandbags!

The tallest and showiest *hāpu'u (C. hawaiense)*, from the Big Island, is used throughout Hawai'i for landscaping and, with other native tree ferns, as a substrate for growing orchids.

Family: Dicksoniaceae
Relatives: Southern hemisphere tree
  ferns
Origin: Hawai'i

This native tree fern *(Cibotium glaucum)* is named for its bluish-white, or glaucous, frond undersides (north slope, Big Island).

APPENDIX

MAJOR BOTANICAL GARDENS AND PARKS IN HAWAI'I

The following is an annotated list of notable locations where trees (native and/or introduced) may be enjoyed and identified in the city or in rural settings. Some areas have labeled trees.

Not every hiking trail, park, picnic area, and nursery (private or otherwise) could be included. The various guides to Hawai'i (general or specific, such as hiking or bicycling), tourist booklets (such as *This Week on Oahu, Maui Gold*), U.S. National Park Service, Sierra Club, The Nature Conservancy, hunting clubs, and others all provide various levels of information.

Particularly helpful for both outdoor enthusiasts and city lovers are publications issued free by the State Department of Land and Natural Resources: *Guide to Hawaii's State Parks* and island maps, which include Forest Reserves, parks, and trails. (To obtain them call area code 808 for all islands plus: O'ahu 548-7455; Maui 244-4354; island of Hawai'i 961-7200; Kaua'i 245-4444). The colored, topographic maps of each island published by University of Hawaii Press and available at bookstores are best.

O'AHU

ALA MOANA PARK: public, free, 76 acres; shade trees and lawn, figs, beachfront; in Waikīkī near Ala Moana Shopping Center.

FOSTER BOTANIC GARDEN: public, fee, 5½ acres; tall, mature, lowland tropical trees (labeled), orchids, palms; Vineyard Boulevard, Honolulu. A beautiful shady spot within the city.

HO'OMALUHIA: public, free, 400 acres; rare tropical trees, Polynesian introduced and native Hawaiian plants, education programs; 160–210 feet elevation; 11 mi. from Honolulu, 7 mi. from Kailua (windward Oahu).

KAPI'OLANI PARK: public, free, 162 acres; shade trees such as showers and banyans; near Waikīkī Aquarium, Waikīkī Shell, and Honolulu Zoo.

KOKO CRATER BOTANIC GARDEN: public, free, 200 acres; dryland tropicals, international; near Hanauma Bay, inside an extinct volcano crater.

LYON ARBORETUM: public, free, 124 acres; 450–1,850 feet elevation; general lush tropical trees (labeled), palms; environmental education; Polynesian and native plants; in Mānoa Valley, 3 mi. inland from H-1 exit at University Avenue.

MOANALUA GARDENS: private, free, 23 acres, 20 feet elevation; spacious lawns, beautifully shaped large monkeypods, general tropical trees; near Pu'uloa/Moanalua Roads on Route 78 (near the airport).

PARADISE PARK: private, fee, 15 acres, 450 feet elevation; lush, mature, lowland tropical trees (labeled), exotic birds, concrete paths, guided tours; near Lyon Arboretum (see above).

WAHIAWĀ BOTANIC GARDEN: public, free, 30 acres, 1,000 feet elevation; tropical trees, palms; California Avenue off Route 80, central O'ahu (near Schofield Barracks).

WAIMEA ARBORETUM: private, fee, 1,800 acres, sea level to 300 feet elevation; lush tropical plants (international), hibiscus, gingers, heliconias, paths, guided tours, educational programs, native birds, everything labeled; historical sites; 60-foot waterfall; 40 mi. from Honolulu, Route 83, north shore near famous surfing beaches (Sunset, etc.).

Also **University of Hawaii Campus** (Mānoa Valley, take University exit off H-1 freeway) and **Haiku Gardens** (Kāne'ohe) on windward O'ahu.

MAUI

ALI'I GARDENS: private, fee, 7 acres, general lowland trees with extensive gingers and heliconias; Hāna Highway near Hāna airport.

HALEAKALĀ NATIONAL PARK: public, fee, sea level to 10,020 feet elevation, 43 square mi.; native subalpine vegetation at upper elevations, moonlike scenery, trails, top of Route 378 (37 mi. upslope from airport); at Kīpahulu end, lush tropical lowland vegetation, spectacular coastal and mountain scenery, trails, high waterfalls; educational programs; 70 mi. along north coast's Hāna Highway from airport.

HĀNA GARDENLAND: private, fee, mostly a nursery but ships tropical trees and palms worldwide; 200 feet elevation; near Hāna airport, 50 mi. east of Kahului.

HELANI GARDENS: private, fee, 70 acres, sea level to 600 feet elevation; extensive lush rainforest vegetation of international tropical foliage, gingers, heliconias, trails or drivethrough; 1 mi. north of Hāna, Hāna Highway.

'IAO VALLEY STATE MONUMENT: public, free, 6 acres; lush mature trees, typical lowland vegetation, streams, spectacular ridges, valleys and mountain peaks adjoining; limited trails; end of 'Iao Valley Road (Route 32).

KE'ANAE ARBORETUM: public, free, 5 acres; tropical trees, Polynesian plants (taro collection), trails, fruit trees, palms, bamboo; 32 mi. east of Kahului on Hāna Highway near Ke'anae YMCA.

KEPANIWAI PARK, 'IAO VALLEY: public, free, 8 acres; especially good for picnics; emphasizes major ethnic groups in Hawai'i with matching architecture and plants (Chinese, Japanese, Portuguese, etc.); en route to 'Iao Valley State Monument.

KULA BOTANICAL GARDEN: private, fee, 5 acres, 3,300 feet elevation; general trees, shrubs, some natives *(koa)*, proteas; stunning views.

MAUI BOTANICAL GARDEN: public, free, 3 acres, sea level; native Hawaiian plants, especially hibiscus, Polynesian introductions; in Kahului at Wailuku Zoo (near Ka'ahumanu Shopping Center, Ka'ahumanu Avenue).

HAWAI'I (BIG ISLAND)

'AKAKA FALLS STATE PARK: public, free, 65 acres; very lush, mostly South American tropical ornamentals and Hawaiian lowland forest; waterfalls up to 442 feet high, heliconias, scenic vistas, trails; on Route 22, 15 mi. north of Hilo near Honomū.

BIRD PARK (KĪPUKA PUAULU): public, free, 100 acres within Hawaii Volcanoes National Park, 4,100 feet elevation; self-guiding nature trail (labeled trees), many rare natives, native birds; 2 mi. west of Volcano House (Route 11 to Mauna Loa Strip Road).

FORESTRY DIVISION TREE NURSERIES: public, free, tropical trees; Kilauea Avenue, Hilo; Waimea (Call the Dept. of Land and Natural Resources, 961-7200).

HAWAI'I TROPICAL BOTANICAL GARDEN: private, fee, 17 acres, sea level; lush tropical forest (primarily exotics), trails, waterfalls; 5 mi. north of Hilo on 4-mile scenic drive near Pepe'ekeo.

HAWAII VOLCANOES NATIONAL PARK: public, fee, 225,000 acres, sea level to 13,667 feet elevation; excellent native forest and tree ferns (especially Thurston Lava Tube), native birds, volcanoes (often active), lava flows; trails, educational programs, information leaflets; 30 mi. southwest of Hilo on Route 11.

KALŌPĀ STATE RECREATION AREA: public, free, 2,000 feet elevation; 0.7-mi. nature hike in native forests and arboretum; near Honoka'a, 50 mi. north of Hilo, off Route 19.

LAVA TREE STATE MONUMENT: public, free, 850 feet elevation; unusual forest of lava molds, native trees; Route 132 (off Route 13), near Pāhoa, 15 mi. south of Hilo.

(QUEEN) LILI'UOKALANI GARDENS: public, free, sea level; spacious lawns with mature ornamental trees, Japanese teahouse, pagodas, palms; Hilo waterfront near Banyan Drive.

MANUKĀ STATE WAYSIDE PARK: public, free, 1,760 feet elevation, 13 acres; native and introduced trees; 41 mi. south of Kona, Route 11. Good picnic spot en route Kona to Hilo via southern route. Also, **Hirose Nurseries, Kong's Floraleigh Gardens, Nani Mau Gardens** (specialty, fruit trees).

KAUA'I

HĀ'ENA STATE PARK (62 acres) and **NĀ PALI COAST STATE PARK** (6,175 acres): these adjoining parks encompass sea level to adjoining mountain precipices, dry and wet vegetation, famous Kalalau Trail along Nā

Pali coast; introduced and native vegetation, spectacular coasts and cliffs.

KŌKEʻE STATE PARK: public, free, 3,600 feet elevation, 4,345 acres; native rainforest (*ʻohiʻa, koa*) and introduced trees; Nuʻalolo-Awaʻawapuhi Trail has labeled trees and booklet; natural history museum, beautiful mountain scenery, hiking trails; Routes 50 and 550, 38 mi. northwest of Līhuʻe.

NATIONAL TROPICAL BOTANICAL GARDEN: private (arranged tours only), 186 acres; beautiful native and introduced mature trees, heliconias; at Lāwaʻi, take Route 53 from Kōloa (southwest of Līhuʻe), left on Hailima Road.

WAIMEA CANYON STATE PARK: public, free, 1,866 acres, to 3,467 feet elevation; native and introduced forests, spectacular gorge and mountain scenery, hiking trails, brochures, some labeled trees; 30 mi. from Līhuʻe (Route 50 west, turn off at Waimea on Route 550).

INDEX

ABOUT THE AUTHOR

Angela Kay Kepler, photographer, field biologist, biological illustrator, and environmental consultant, holds degrees from the University of Canterbury, University of Hawaii, and Cornell University and was a post-doctoral student at Oxford University. She is the author of a dozen books, among them *Hawaiian Heritage Plants*, *Proteas in Hawaii*, and guides to Maui's Hāna Highway and Haleakalā.

She visited one of the most remote atolls in the Pacific on a Soviet-American joint expedition in 1988, and in 1990 she was a scientific co-leader for the Line and Phoenix Islands Expedition, conducting comprehensive surveys of seabirds and terrestrial ecosystems in the Central Pacific Ocean.